Chameleon: The Poacher's Enemy

Brandon Kimbrough

Dedication

This book is dedicated to all the animals in the world that are endangered and have gone extinct.

To all the animal rights activists and organizations that help fight for the well-being of animals.

This book is also dedicated to all animal lovers around the world.

About the Author

Brandon Kimbrough was born in Spartanburg, South Carolina. He has always had affection for animals, and it started as a young child when he would bring home stray and wounded animals and then care for them. His big imagination began when he was in elementary school where he found writing stories as a passion. Being creative has always been his strong suit. He strongly believes that with faith and great determination all things are possible. In his spare time, he enjoys water-related activities and hiking.

Preface

This book has been written to bring awareness about the world of illegal poaching and inspire people to help save these animals, prone to illegal poaching, from extinction. My goal is for animals to be able to cohabitate in their environment in peace. (In other words, leave them alone)

Contents

Dedication...i

About the Author..ii

Preface...iii

Chapter 1: Trip to the Safari..1

Chapter 2: The Pain..20

Chapter 3: The Veterinarian...40

Chapter 4: King Poacher..54

Chapter 5: Tech Support..69

Chapter 6: At the Bottom...87

Chapter 7: In the Jungles..102

Chapter 8: Rescue..122

Chapter 9: Hunted..138

Chapter 10: Disbanded..153

Chapter 11: Is It Enough?..171

Chapter 12: The Poaching Party...188

Chapter 13: Abandoned..206

Chapter 14: One on One...225

Chapter 15: The Aftermath..245

Page Left Blank Intentionally

Chapter 1: Trip to the Safari

It was an ordinary start of an ordinary day in a young man's life. While growing up, we all have a certain vision — a certain perspective of the world around us. When we are young, our parents teach us to always think positively. We are taught to never think badly of anyone or anything. Most of all, we are taught to always look at the bright side.

As children, we are blessed with something that most adults crave later in their lives. It is something they covet, something that makes them long for the old days of childhood when they could run around the backyard, play with dolls, and pretend like life was all roses and sunshine. As children, we are blessed with the beauty of innocence that blinds us to the truths of the world. We do not have the mental ability to discern right from wrong, what is authentic, and what is fake. As kids, we always think that it is either black or white while ignoring the gray parts of life.

Once upon a time, there was an intelligent man. His mind was always full of ideas. One day, he proposed that we are born with a veil covering our mental vision. We grow up into toddlers, then adolescents, and then, finally, adults. However, as we grow older and older, that veil starts to lift gradually. Our vision starts to become sharper, our gaze more pronounced, and our mind a little less innocent and a lot more open. While growing up, we tend to believe that everything we see is real. Or even when we don't see something, we believe it when our parents say that Santa Claus will bring us presents. We believe it when our teacher says that coloring within the lines is an important skill.

We also believe the stories and fairytales, showing us a world where everything and everyone is either good or bad. No in-between.

As Ben grew up, he had many thoughts, ideas, and wild imaginations, just like any other child of his age. Sure, his life was a little different, a lot less troubled, and definitely more comfortable than many. However, he was still born with that same veil we all are born with. He had the innocence that we all crave once we lose it to our adulthoods. Ben was born with the best blessing of all — faith. He always believed that no matter what happened, good always wins in the end.

Every time his parents would read him a bedtime story, his faith was reaffirmed and he would go to sleep dreaming about good vanquishing evil. He would hear stories of princes taking down dragons, monsters, and even evil kings. That was what he grew up with. So, it made sense that Ben always believed that in the fight of good versus bad, good always wins. No matter what.

Another thing that Ben grew up with was a strong will. Ever since he was little, his parents would comment on how Ben never gave up on things he wanted. He would tell them about how he wanted to be a superhero. His parents and other adults around him would simply pat him on the back, coo at his adorableness, and commend how his innocence didn't seem to go away. They knew that it was not impossible because none of this was true, they knew that superheroes are fake, but to little Ben, good was able to conquer any bad. So, he always imagined himself growing up and becoming a strong superhero who would fight for good and defeat the bad.

There was once a time when Ben got into a fight with a student at his preschool. He was very young at the time and never had gotten into a fight before. Ben was not an aggressive child. He was always the calmer and more collected one. "An old soul," as his mother liked to call him. So, for Ben to get into a fight was something that was completely unexpected for his parents. When they got a call from the principal, they didn't know whether to be scared or extremely worried. As they made their way over to the school, they couldn't help but wonder what had gotten into their son to make him behave so unlike himself.

As they reached Ben's school, they witnessed the two boys standing side by side along with Principal Meyers. Their clothes were wrinkled and dirty, marked with dirt stains from the muddy playground of the school. Their hair was a mess, and their faces wore expressions of petulance and guilt. Ben's parents were shocked by the sight that they were greeted with. They had never seen Ben in such a state before.

"Principal Meyers, hello," Ben's dad greeted.

The principal held out her hand to greet them and then led them back into her office. The children were told to stand outside while the principal talked to the parents. When Ben's parents walked inside the office, they noticed another older couple waiting inside.

"These are Mike Camper's parents," Principal Meyers introduced.

After the parents greeted each other in a terse manner, considering the circumstances, the principal got right down to the topic

"Right, so," Principal Meyers said as she took her seat in the chair behind her desk.

The parents waited anxiously to hear what she had to say.

"You all know the reason why you are called here today," Principal Meyers continued. "Mike and Ben were caught fighting in the playground today after school. A teacher had to literally pull them off each other."

Ben's mom gasped at the knowledge.

"When we asked what had happened, Ben only had one explanation. He said that Mike hurt his friend," Principal Meyers explained.

"That's preposterous! Mike has never hurt a child before!" Mike's mother exploded.

"And you think Ben has?!" Ben's father responded.

"Please, let's not lose our cool over this. I just want to discuss this with you so that it doesn't occur again. Ben and Mike are both exceptional students, and we've never had any complaints about their conduct before. That is why we were all surprised to see two of our most docile and polite students fighting it out on the playground," Principal Meyers said.

"Which friend of Ben did Mike hurt, Principal Meyers?" Ben's mother asked, trying to cut down the tension in the room.

"That's the thing. He's not telling us," Principal Meyers said.

After that, the principal called the boys in to explain their side of the story.

"Ben, would you like to explain to your parents and Mike's parents what happened in the playground today?" Principal Meyers asked.

Ben stumbled through an explanation, saying the same thing that the principal had said.

"Ben," Ben's father called for him. "Which friend of yours did Mike hurt?"

"Keele," Ben mumbled.

"Who is Keele?" Ben's mother asked.

"He's the groundskeeper's bloodhound," Ben mumbled.

For a moment, the silence that wrapped around the room and its occupants was thick enough to be its own entity.

"Ben," Principal Meyers started. "Are you saying that the friend Mike hurt, the one whom you hurt Mike for, was ... the groundskeeper's dog?"

The confusion was apparent in the principal's voice and the barely concealed expressions on the faces of the parents.

"Yes! He's so sweet and loves to play with us. Mike threw a rock at him, and it hurt him in the eye!" Ben exclaimed, not looking sorry at all.

Principal Meyers' eyes widened, "Ben...."

"Did you hurt our son for a *dog*?!" Mike's mother exclaimed.

"Mrs. Camper, please refrain from yelling at a child," Principal Meyers said sternly, then she turned toward Ben. "Ben, is that true?"

"Of course!" Ben said matter-of-factly.

Ben's parents just looked down and shook their heads in disbelief. They sighed and stood up.

"I am so sorry, Mr. and Mrs. Camper. I can't believe it. Actually, I can believe that Ben would do something like that, but I am still sorry," Ben's mother said.

"No, you shouldn't apologize," Mike's dad said. "Mike, why did you hurt a dog? We've talked about this."

Mike received a stern scolding from his parents that day and a lecture on how to not hurt animals. Meanwhile, Ben learned the lesson that he couldn't exactly act out his superhero tendencies when it came to protecting animals.

"But, who will protect them if not me?" Ben asked his father that night.

The veil of his innocence was particularly apparent that night.

"Because, Ben," his father sighed, "there are times when you cannot fight for every innocent being. I know it seems like the right thing to do, but see how you got into trouble for it. Violence is never the answer, son. You should never have to resort to that."

That was the day Ben's father tried to lift Ben's veil a little, but it didn't work. Ben was set in his ways. He refused to believe that fighting for the good side could ever be bad or not work out in the end.

***

Ben sat under the bright summer sun, half under the shade of a big palm tree as a soft, warm breeze wafted. He looked up and squinted against the sharp sun rays. The warmth felt good against his skin. He closed his eyes, seeing a red haze behind his closed eyelids. He stood up and started walking. In his hands were his little toy animals. There was a tyrannosaurus rex, a zebra, and a blue whale. It is an odd combination but one that Ben had chosen on his own.

"Ben! Darling, come inside. Your mom is looking for you!" ordered a voice from inside.

"Coming, Mom. Gimme a minute," replied Ben. He turned away and continued engaging his toy animals in a fight.

Ben had a vivid imagination. Today, he and his animals were fighting off an evil alien overlord that had decided to attack the Earth. With the power of friendship, Ben and his animals — a flame-breathing dinosaur, a flying zebra, and a mighty whale — quickly vanquished their foes. Emerging victorious, they celebrated by having a nice, little dinner in their castle. Their party was cut short when reality kicked in and Ben was forced to abandon his team.

"Come on in, Ben!" Mom called out, louder now. She sounded annoyed, and that meant it was time for Ben to be on his way.

Disgruntled, Ben dragged his feet and slid the garden door open. He trudged across the hallway, bringing in dirt and grass with him. Before his mom could see that, he ran upstairs and jumped into the shower. Turning the faucets, he could hear his mother complaining about the mess.

"Benjamin! I am tired of you always making this mess. You best believe this shower gives you super strength because I'm going to beat your ass!" his mother said.

Ben wasn't worried. His mother could be tough, but he was sure she loved him more than anything.

"I didn't raise you to raise hell!" She would say. She emphasized good manners and didn't stand for unruliness. Ben behaved for the most part, and the only time he went against her rule was when he played outside.

Playing with his animals outside was the highlight of Ben's day. There was nothing more important to him than to grab his three favorite toys, go outside, and have a blast—all on his own. He could create a world, populate it with all sorts of interesting characters, and amuse himself like no one else. So far, he had fought aliens, defeated a dictator, and discovered a new planet. Any bizarre and unreal situation he could cook up, Ben would go on to experience it with his animals.

Ben was this way ever since he was a little baby.

His first toy was a plushy gorilla named Peter, who he would lug around everywhere he went. For the first few years of his life, wherever Ben went, Peter went with him. Hours would go by, and Ben and Peter would keep each other company, having the time of their lives. But then, one night, Ben forgot Peter outside the house. That night, it rained cats and dogs. The next morning when his father discovered Peter, he was damaged beyond repair. Being soaked all night in the pouring rain and then clawed at in the morning by birds, his fur was ripped. The cotton inside was all over the place. Ben's parents knew he would crumble if he saw Peter this way, so they made up a story.

"You know how you live with your mom and dad, huh, Ben?" his mom asked him.

"Uh-huh," Ben nodded, clueless about where this would lead.

"Well, Peter's parents missed him. So they came over in the middle of the night...." his mom added.

"And they took him back home," his dad finished.

"Nooo!" Ben cried.

An endless onslaught of tears and tantrums followed. However, the kindness in Ben's heart took over soon, and he eventually understood. "Peter is with his parents," he'd hiccup when his mom asked him if he was okay and if he still missed Peter. No more than four years old at the time, he was bamboozled into believing that his toy friend had left him for better pastures. Little did he know that the poor thing had been ravaged like a gazelle in the Serengeti.

To compensate for this tragic and untimely loss, his father took him to a toy store a few miles from home. Ben was allowed to get whatever he wanted. After going around for the best part of half an hour, Ben picked up three animals.

"Why these?" His father asked, confused.

"They like me. I like them," Ben quipped.

Even though he was a well-mannered kid, he had a witty side to him. His humor often had all of his family members in fits of laughter. It wasn't about him saying something extraordinarily funny. It was just the randomness of his wit that got everybody in stitches.

Ben's mother, Mary, was a housewife. She had married his father, Christopher Morrison, at a young age. Being high school sweethearts, the two of them stuck together through thick and thin. Mary waited for Christopher, or Chrissy Poo as she teased him, to get done with college. Once he did, he asked her father for his daughter's hand in marriage. Chris and Mary got married to each other at the young age of 23. They spent the next few years focusing on their careers. She was a florist, and he was a veterinarian. When his practice took off and they had their children, she decided that she was going to focus on her family. Christopher made more than enough money to provide for everyone. First came Ben's older sister Mel, then brother Kit, and finally, it was Ben. Their family was their sanctuary. It was a tight-knit unit.

Christopher's career took off, and not too long after his big breakout, he began investing his earnings in other businesses. With a friend, he formed a partnership at a carwash. With his father-in-law, he bought a share of his car dealership. All of this meant that Ben and his family lived relatively peaceful lives. There were times when an argument would sprout up here or there, but it was never a big deal. So Ben only knew peace, love, and warmth.

To make matters better, Ben's grandparents were always a key part of his life. Both of his mother's parents were alive. His paternal grandfather was around when his siblings were born but he passed away shortly before Ben came into the world. He had been a long-time smoker who had fallen prey to cancer. It progressed a lot faster than it could be treated, and before everyone knew it, he was gone. When Ben was born, Christopher's grief somewhat subsided. In his baby boy, Christopher saw his father. They had the same big, brown eyes and stubby nose. Ben was named after his grandfather to honor his memory.

Coming up was a trip that Ben's father had been planning for a few years. It would involve Ben's parents, siblings, and one of his grandparents. The whole group would fly to Africa, where they would travel to different places and take in the entire Safari experience. Ben was jumping with joy when he heard that he was going to Africa. Up until now, he had only seen it all on the channel Animal Planet, but this was the first time that he was going to see it in person. It was a dream come true. Knowing how much his son loved all things related to animals, Christopher made sure the travel plan involved all outdoor activities, like horse riding, feeding animals, etc. He wanted to make sure his family and especially his baby boy had a good time. Preparations for this trip took some time because he had to make sure someone could fill in for him at work. All of this planning and preparation took everyone a few weeks.

Ben and his father were extremely close—almost inseparable. While his older siblings were more self-sufficient and would willingly want to be independent, Ben loved to be pampered. His parents treated all of their children equally, but Ben always wanted to be shown love the most. This support from his parents, the presence of grandparents, and a generally stable household meant that Ben grew up as a kind and compassionate person.

Everyone acknowledged Ben's kindness and compassion. All of his teachers in school knew him as the nicest kid in the classroom. Although shy, he was always ready to help everyone. His grades were always good, and he was loved by everybody. However, despite all of this, the only person he really got along with was his friend Dylan. Dylan was Ben's classmate. He had curly, brown hair and wide, dark eyes. He always dressed as flamboyantly as possible. His palette ranged from neon green to pastel pink and everything in between. This was due to his mother, who was a graduate of fashion design school. She always mixed and matched different things for her brand. She would try all her experiments with colors and textures on her little boy Dylan. Initially, she did it for fun, but when she saw that Dylan also had a knack for it, she kept going.

Ben and Dylan first met in kindergarten. Ben was sitting alone on his first day, seeing which Dylan came and sat down next to him. With a squeaky voice, he extended his hand.

"Hi! My name is Dylan. Wanna be friends?"

Ben knew no one else, so he was glad that Dylan had initiated the conversation. He silently nodded in agreement, and that was the start of something beautiful.

Since then, the two were an inseparable duo. They did everything together. In addition to his animals, Ben considered Dylan his best friend. If Ben wasn't playing with animals or family or wasn't studying, he was with Dylan. Ben's parents had befriended Dylan's mom, and the two boys would always be at each other's homes. They went from kiddy pool parties to choosing college together and everything in between.

Dylan's family was not too different than Ben's. The only difference was that his father had laid down his life for his country. He had been a marine, and, on one mission, he was on the wrong end of a sniper's scope. The bullet tore through his chest, and while he was able to get to a hospital, he eventually succumbed to the injury. Dylan had a blurred memory of his father, but that was all about it. All of this had happened when he was probably three or four years old. Dylan's mother had made sure her son was a headstrong and determined individual who didn't need anyone else. She instilled into him a work ethic that made him very hardworking. Ben and he would always be the first two names on the list when it came to the best students in the class.

Perhaps the biggest and strongest link of their friendship was their shared love for animals. The two boys were obsessed with all things related to animals. Ben and Dylan both had a pet goldfish. Dylan named his fish Ben and Ben named his Dylan. This way, even if the two weren't together, they were.

Ben loved his pet fish. He sat on his writing table, and while doing his homework, he would have short conversations with Dylan, the fish. He would tell him about his entire day, confide in him, and make sure he was always fed. Like his namesake, Dylan the fish was Ben's best buddy.

Next to Dylan, the fish, was a cage with Louis, the hamster. Louis was a gift from Ben's grandmother for his birthday. He was an adorable, little, fluffy hamster with light-brown fur and two large white patches around his eyes. During the day, Louis would constantly be rustling around his little cage, drinking water out of his little bowl, and eating the fruits that Ben would feed him. At night, Louis would burn all of these calories by running around his little wheel. The squeaking of his wheel would be the only sound at night.

Hearing this, Ben would know that all was well and good in his life. The sounds would always calm him down. There was not much that Ben loved more than his pet animals. They were his world, and he was ready to go to any length to make sure they were safe and healthy.

After Ben got out of the shower, his mom called out to him, "Benny! Dylan's here!"

"Oh, Dylan's here!" Ben said, jumping with excitement. He ran through the hallway and skipped down the stairs, spotting Dylan sitting on the large sofa that almost swallowed him whole.

"Hiya!" Dylan said.

"Hiya!" Ben said, saluting him. This was a new trick the boys had come up with.

Ben's mom watched the two boys from a distance, shaking her head and smiling. Secretly, she was glad that Ben had found someone his age to hang out with. He was a somewhat-quiet child outside of the home and took his sweet time letting people close. So when he and Dylan became such fast friends, both she and Christopher heaved a sigh of relief. They didn't want their little boy to suffer from loneliness. Sure, Ben had his toy animals and pets to keep him company, but it was important to make friends with people like yourself.

"Dylan, honey, want some lemonade?"

"Sure, Mrs. Morrison!" Dylan beamed up at her.

"Ben, don't you go dripping all over the floor. Go and dry off your hair," Mary instructed and headed inside the kitchen.

"Mom!" Ben whispered, exasperated. "Gimme a minute," he said to Dylan and rushed into his room. He quickly dried his hair and turned around to leave the room. He was excited to tell Dylan all about the upcoming Safari trip. At the last minute, he grabbed his blue whale and exited the room. He ran down to Dylan, who was already halfway through his lemonade.

"Dylan! Did I tell you about the trip?"

"Man, that's all you have been talking about for months!" Dylan said, laughing. He scrunched up his nose and turned away.

"Ha-ha! Dylan, I know you wanna know all the details about it. Hey, come on up. We'll go to my room, and I'll show you all the stuff Dad has got."

"Let's go!" Dylan turned toward Ben and grinned. The two of them dashed to Ben's room.

"These are my sneakers!" Ben announced, holding up hip red sneakers.

"Wow, pretty cool!" Dylan commented.

"And these flip-flops," Ben thrust the sandals almost into Dylan's nose.

Dylan backed away, laughing. "But what do you need these for?" he demanded.

Ben shrugged, "Dunno. Dad said we need flip-flops there to walk around comfortably. Maybe for the pools or something."

"Grown-ups have got strange ideas," Dylan mused.

"They sure do," Ben said, distracted. He walked to and fro in his room, going from the wardrobe to the shelf.

"What are you looking for?" Dylan demanded after a few moments of observing Ben spinning through the room like a top.

Just then, Ben squealed, "There is it!"

"What?"

"My binoculars!"

"Wow!" Dylan let out a whistle.

"Cool, huh? I have never seen something so cool before, Dylan," Ben said, extending the binoculars toward Dylan for him to hold and admire.

"It's just like in the movies. You know the kind people use to watch stuff in the far-off distance," Dylan commented, sticking his eyes to the two lenses and training the binoculars in Ben's direction.

"Your nose looks so big!" Dylan guffawed.

Ben opened his mouth then flared his nostril, stepping closer to Dylan.

Both boys burst out laughing.

"You looked really funny," Dylan hiccupped, handing the binoculars back to Ben.

"That's 'cause I am," Ben said, wriggling his brows.

"What else have you got?"

"This is pretty much it. Dad and mom have got the rest. They have these huge bags."

"How huge?" Dylan asked.

"Very! They have all the clothes in them for all of us. I saw some meds too, and some bundles of socks and bathrobes and other stuff are there too. Dad even packed his big camera for the trip. So I guess we'll have a lot of pictures."

"Sounds like fun," Dylan said wistfully.

Ben walked over to Dylan and put his arm around him. "I wish you could come with me, too."

"Me too," Dylan said, pouting. "But I guess I can't leave mom here all by herself."

Ben added, "You gotta stay back and take care of her."

"And you take a lot of pictures and then show them to me," Dylan said.

"I promise," Ben nodded his head solemnly. "This will be the best trip ever!" He growled, pumping his fist in the air.

"Best trip!" Dylan shouted back.

The two boys giggled at each other and began to jump on the bed, knowing no one was around to keep an eye on them or stop them from turning Ben's bed into a trampoline.

Did you know?

Illegal wildlife trafficking is a business worth $5–$23 billion a year.

Chapter 2: The Pain

The time for the safari was coming thick and fast. Excitement levels were high. Ben and Dylan were giddy beyond control. For them, being able to be around animals that they had only ever seen on TV or in books was too much to handle. There were a lot of little things that needed to be ironed out, and it was being handled by Ben's parents.

Ben's father had a cousin who worked in the booking department for the safaris. He had managed to squeeze them into this because there was a waiting list that went on for several months. Seeing animals in their natural habitat was simply amazing. It meant seeing their biggest hobby, their biggest dream coming true right in front of them. There was little that came close to their excitement, and they did no job of hiding it.

"Dylan ... Dylan ... Guess what!"

"What? What? What is it, Ben?"

"I read that there are going to be giraffes, lions, and even leopards if we are lucky! You know all of these animals are on the endangered animals' list?"

Dylan didn't know what this was. On his face was a look of confusion.

"Wha ... What list?"

"See, let me explain this to you. There are some animals who are everywhere, like cows, goats, and zebras. There are a lot of these animals. But! And this is a big *but*! There are a lot of animals whose numbers are tumbling. These animals used to be in the hundreds of thousands, but now just a few are surviving."

"But why? What's happening to them? Are they getting sick? Are they running away?"

"Well, in a way, yeah," replied Ben. His point was beginning to take shape.

"Poaching. These animals are being hunted down and killed, and their body parts are used by people who are cruel enough to do so. Do you know they make carpets out of their skin? They'll catch a leopard or a tiger, kill it, skin it, and make a carpet out of its skin. The worse thing is, they even stick their heads on a wall! You know what they call this?"

Dylan, disgusted, had shock plastered across his face. Up until now, all that he had known was that wild animals roam free, and nothing happens to them. The thought of humans killing these animals for fun was something far beyond his understanding. He couldn't wrap his head around this. To him, this was something out of this world.

As a young boy, Dylan was pretty average and simple. He didn't feel like he was an extraordinary kid, like Ben. Ben had always been extraordinary. He was always getting the best grades, excelling in all the extracurricular activities and being a model kid for all parents. Dylan had become best friends with Ben a long time ago, but he still found it odd that they had become best friends because Dylan was nothing like Ben. Sure, they shared a few interests, but they were very different people.

Dylan had grown up in a relatively happier household. He never had to complain or want anything since his parents provided him with a good and comfortable life. He was not a straight A's student, something his parents wished he would emulate from his best friend. He wasn't bad at studies, but he just didn't like it much. He would rather play soccer and catch slugs all day, instead of studying. Ben was a bookworm and loved studying. He was always excited whenever they received a project in school. The boys would team up and work on it together, but Ben would always take the lead.

Dylan didn't mind Ben being in charge of most things in their friendship, since he knew Ben was smarter than him. He knew that if Ben did something, then it would turn out better. In simple terms, Ben was the smart one and Dylan was the athletic one. They both had aspects in which they excelled. It was something they both knew and sometimes took advantage of as well.

Dylan remembered there was once an older boy in their school who was bullying them. Ben and Dylan would always get cornered by the boy and his group of friends in the hallways after lunch. They didn't know what to do. Ben would just tell Dylan that they could just forget about it and move on. Dylan was fine with that, until the day the bullies stole their lunch.

"Really? PB&J sandwiches? What are you, five?" Bart said, his friends snickering along with him.

Dylan glared at the bully, staying silent as per Ben's advice. He wanted to smack the boy, but he knew he shouldn't. Ben was also silent, but his fists were clenched. Then he spoke up.

"That's his lunch. Give it back to him," Ben said in a calm, yet low voice.

Bart shared a look with his friends and then they all started laughing.

"His lunch? Really? Will he cry if I took it?" Bart said as they continued to laugh.

Ben stopped Dylan before he could pounce on the older guy and said, "Please, you can't take his lunch."

"I think I can, little wart," Bart said smugly.

Then he and his friends sauntered away, with Dylan's lunch in hand.

"Ben?! What the hell?! Why didn't you let me at him?!" Dylan yelled at Ben.

"Oh, because you could've taken them on all by yourself, or could you?" Ben asked sarcastically.

"I wouldn't have gone down without a fight at least! Now, he's gonna think we're wusses!" Dylan said.

"Who cares what he thinks? He's a bully. Come on, don't be upset. I saved you from getting your butt kicked," Ben said.

Dylan looked down and sighed, "Yeah, you're probably right."

Ben patted Dylan on the shoulder and grabbed his arm to lead him to the cafeteria. "Come on, let's go have lunch. I'll share."

Since that day, Dylan always listened to his smart best friend. He knew that Ben had his back and would always help him out. However, he wasn't done with the bullies yet. They stole his lunch, and that was an unforgivable offense in Dylan's eyes. That night, he called Ben and they talked about how to get revenge on the bullies. Dylan wanted to just fight them, but Ben told him how fighting would never work with bullies like Bart. A little while later, Ben called Dylan and told him of a plan he had thought of at dinner. It involved his mother's famous roast beef steak sandwiches. They were all set for the revenge they had planned on the bullies.

The next day, Ben and Dylan stood in the lone hallway before lunch. Just as the group of the bullies rounded the corner, Dylan started talking about his lunch, loudly.

"Oh, man! I can't wait to have these roast beef steak sandwiches my mom packed me today! They're so good!" Dylan said.

Ben played along, "Yeah, I'll take a bite, too. I bet it's amazing!"

The bullies came to them, just as the boys had planned. After their normal routine of pushing the boys into the lockers and making fun of their hair or clothes, Bart said, "So, you brought some fancy lunch today, huh?"

Dylan tried to protect his backpack but Bart was faster.

"Uh-huh. You can't enjoy these all by yourself," Bart snickered along with his friends.

Dylan and Ben remained silent, suffering the harassment until Bart finally walked away with Dylan's lunch as planned.

"For how long do these laxatives work?" Dylan whispered to Ben.

"In an hour or so," Ben replied.

An hour later, Ben and Dylan went to see where the bullies were. They noticed the group of older boys, all running through the busy and packed hallway toward the bathroom. The class had just ended.

"Move it!"

"Coming through!"

"Get out of my way!"

Bart and his friends were clutching their stomachs and trying to run to the bathrooms. Bart stumbled and fell on the floor in his haste. Then suddenly, the loud and chaotic hallway fell silent as a loud fart broke through the noise. Everyone looked at the red-faced Bart lying on the floor, and then hell broke loose. Everyone started laughing as Bart tried to get up and rush to the bathroom.

Ben and Dylan held their stomachs from laughing so hard at the sight. Ben had come up with a plan to add laxatives to the sandwiches so that the bullies would get a taste of their own medicine. Literally. That was the day Dylan realized that Ben was the perfect partner for him. He couldn't have asked for a better best friend for himself if he tried.

The two best friends knew since that day that their friendship was of power, as they could both apply their skills in certain situations. Ben was always the level-headed one, the one coming up with smart ideas while Dylan would carry those plans out. Dylan knew that his best friend always wanted to become a superhero, but he never laughed at his dreams. If anyone could do it, Dylan knew it would be Ben.

Their love for animals was just another thing that brought them closer. Ben always loved animals, and when he caught Dylan catching slugs and keeping them in a safe environment, he knew he had found his best friend. They would always pet any dog or cat they saw on the street, play with any animal that found them, and generally look for fun facts about animals. Their favorite Halloween costumes were also animals. They would pick their favorite animal of that year and dress up like that.

It was only recently that Ben had started dressing up as endangered animals. He would dress up as a panda, tiger, whale, etc. At first, Dylan didn't know the reason behind Ben's actions — not until he explained it to him one day. At the time, Dylan pretended to understand what Ben meant by "endangered animals." He didn't want to seem like he didn't know some important term regarding animals, since he knew a lot. However, today was the day that Dylan finally confessed his lack of knowledge on the subject.

"What do they ca ... call it?" Dylan stuttered.

"A trophy! Like doing any of this is an achievement. I swear, Dylan, when I found out about this, I cried my eyes out. Knowing that there are people who want to harm animals like this makes me so angry."

Teeth grinding, sweat trickling, nerves unsettling, Ben was mad. With a heart, pure to its core, the little boy could not wrap his head around the fact that there are people who actually do this. These weren't animals who were harming people. These were animals who were minding their own business. And people would go to them and kill them. Ben was pacing up and down the length of his room. Dylan had his head lowered. The two young boys, livid as one could be, were trying to compose themselves.

"You see, Ben! This is why I always tell everyone around me that animals and humans should be treated the same."

"Right, Dylan, you're so right!"

"Animals are beautiful creatures of nature. They come in so many different shapes, sizes, colors, all over the world. It's amazing. I could live to be as old as possible and still not see every animal there is. I mean, we've only seen ten percent of the oceans, and there are still some parts on land."

Dylan's eyes glistened. Ben's eyes had a fire burning in them. The two boys, driven by their love for animals, loved this conversation. They were having the best time talking about it, but when they looked down at their watches, it was half past nine.

Ben's family was to leave the next morning, and it was going to be the trip of their lifetime. As per their plan, the two families were going to fly across the globe to the plains of Africa. It was an early morning flight, and things needed to be taken care of. Ben didn't have to do anything, but his parents didn't have all the time in the world. Packing was done. Tickets were ready. Everything was ready. Now, the only thing left was to get there.

The following morning, both Dylan and Ben's family met at the airport, exchanged pleasantries, and made their way to their planes. It was a long flight ahead, and the kids spent the most part of it sleeping, saving up the energy that they needed to have fun on the safari. There was one flight that got them to Nairobi, the place where they spent the entire day adjusting to the local time. That night, they ordered room service and had several laughs. Ben was excited to finally take the safari, as was the rest of the family. For most of them, this was the first time that they had even been to this part of the world, let alone gone on a safari.

The next morning, Ben's family was to be picked up from their hotel by the safari staff and then taken to the park. It was a natural park that had been set up by the local government for the preservation of local species because of the rampant poaching that was going on. The animal population had been diminishing for years, and the black-market trade was booming. Rich people in the middle east, far east, and Americas were big fans of things like elephant tusks, leopard skins, and lion paws.

The local poachers were paid thousands of dollars every time they were tasked to find a specific animal. This was quick and easy money for them, and in a place where a lot of people struggle to make ends meet, they were willing to go to any length to get the job done. As a result of this, the once-flourishing local wildlife had been ravaged to the point where most people feared that they would be wiped out. Had the government not taken the initiative, these poachers would probably go through the entire population.

To get to this park, a drive that was no less than two hours was required. It was early in the morning, and despite the excitement that came along with it, it wasn't easy to get up. Having to wake up at six in the morning at a time when your sleep schedule is already all over the place was not the best feeling. Nonetheless, Ben was up—bright and early. He had barely gotten any sleep all night but was somehow showing no signs of it.

"Mel! Kit!" Ben called out his siblings.

"Bennn!" replied an equally excited Mel.

Dressed in khaki safari suits, Ben and his sibling wore matching outfits. It was going to be a bright, sunny, and hot day, so they needed to dress the part. Their parents all wore thin clothes because the inevitable wave of heat and sweat was going to make life very difficult.

After convening in the hotel lobby, Ben's family made sure they had everything that was needed. His dad made a list, i.e. bug spray, first-aid kit, bottled water, ropes, and hats; these were the things that they were required to arrange for themselves while the tour group was going to do the rest. They had paid good money for this safari and were expecting it to be worth every penny. Despite this, they were told that there was a very real risk of something deadly happening if the animals are pestered. The guys could lose their life. If that does happen, the tour operators will not be liable for the damage. They would help in any way they could, but this was all happening with the consent of the guests. This was such a big deal that the tour company had made the family sign an affidavit that confirmed this.

Seeing how far this was taken, Ben's mother, Mary, had her reservations.

"Jesus, this is really something. Are we sure we want to do this?" She said worriedly.

"Well, you're not wrong, but we can' let that ruin the trip. It's taken a lot to get here, and I don't really think that there is a chance for us to go back now. Is there?" replied Ben's father.

Mary's mother shrugged it off and checked to see if she had everything that was needed. The others did the same, and in the meantime, their transportation arrived. It was a large Toyota Coaster bus that could seat at least 25 people. Walking out of the hotel lobby, everyone was hit in the face by a fiercely hot, wafting breeze. It was dry, and they felt as if it was piercing their skin.

They rushed onto the bus, which was nice and air-conditioned. The family was used to warm weather, but this was something different. As opposed to the warm weather back home, this was hot and sticky. It choked your neck, and your skin felt like it was covered in dirt. Making a brief stroll from the lobby to the bus, both families already felt the hard end of the stick. The air-conditioning did its job, and, within a few moments, they were all cooled down.

This was the beginning of what was going to be an incredibly eventful trip. One that was going to change their lives forever. The bus driver was a young man dressed in a crisp white shirt and black dress pants.

"Hello, all! Welcome. I hope you're all excited about your safari. I promise you; this is going to be life-changing!" announced the bus driver.

This had everyone excited, and the mood on the bus was joyous. Everyone was singing along to the music that the driver put on. It was a playlist of Steven Tyler, Michael Jackson, ACDC, and Bruce Springsteen. Being so far from home yet finding music that they knew was something that made the start of the trip even better. Ben and his father were huge fans of Steven Tyler. They absolutely loved his persona and would sing his songs all day long. Ben had even managed to make Mel get in on the craze.

Singing, dancing, and having a good time was how the entire bus drive went. It took them a while to get there, but once they did, they were blown away. In order to get to the park, they drove along a highway. It was a regular highway to the point where they began seeing large fences.

"This is where the park begins! All of this is protected. The animals are the government's property, and no one is allowed to harm any of them. It is illegal for anyone to hunt any of them, and there is a long stay in jail for those who do," explained the bus driver, turning around and giving a wide grin to everyone. It was almost as if he knew that something was going to happen and was trying his best to hide it.

The whole group looked around, trying to take in the sights.

"Oh, my goodness, Ben! Look! Look outside the window!" yelled Kit.

When Ben turned his head to take a look, there was a herd of wildebeest that was gathered, grazing. This was the first time that anyone had seen something like this, and everyone was blown away. Ben was beyond himself. He stood up against the window, his arms plastered across the big glass windows.

Driving forward, the bus turned off the main road and down a dirt track that led to a large house. This was where they were going to disembark from the bus, get ready, and go out onto the plains.

"Mom! Did you see that? Wasn't it so damn cool!" screeched Ben, unable to contain himself.

"Ben! Language!" his father complained. "It's normal to be excited, but that isn't a ticket for language like that. Not at all."

"Oh, sorry," frowned Ben, knowing that he had messed up.

The next step was for them to make sure they had their supplies and the right clothes on, and it was also for the security team to be ready. While this was supposed to be a joyous ride, these were real animals in their natural habitat. At any point in time, they could attack, and there was usually one end to that story.

Even if it wasn't a lion that attacked, other animals weren't as cute or cuddly either. A single wildebeest can rip through a grown man using just its horns. One kick from a zebra and you best believe you're making a one-way trip to the cemetery. These were not animals from your petting zoo; these were wild beasts that needed to be treated as such.

The security team in question had five men. Tall and broad, these men had matching gray uniforms on and had rifles hanging by their side.

"Dad, what is that? Why do those men have guns?" asked Ben.

Shuffling around, his father didn't know how to respond.

"Honey, those guns are only to scare away the bad animals. If a mean lion wants to come and take a bite of you, these men will tell it not to," replied his mother.

His father breathed a sigh of relief.

Meanwhile, the jeeps were ready, and the drivers were waiting. These were repurposed jeep wranglers that had been made specifically for safaris. They had a large cage on them— no windows and no windshield. Open from all sides, the only thing protecting the group was a cage that had been soldered onto the body of the jeeps.

Roaring to life, these jeeps blew out thick clouds of black smoke from behind them. This was not encouraging, but it was all they had. It was all they were going to get, whether they liked it or not.

Once the safari began, that was when the real fun started. Kicking all the dust in their way, the two jeeps made their way across the mighty planes. On both sides of them was the wild and untamed African bush. It was truly spectacular. As far as the eye could see, there were trees, wild grass, and different animals all frolicking around.

Driving past a herd of zebras and wildebeests, everyone was amazed to finally see them in the flesh. This was the first time that this had happened, and it was something that was truly remarkable. Ben was a menace to restrain. This was a dream come true for him, and he was going to make sure he savored every bit of it. Out of the seats and against the cages, he couldn't help but jump out of the car. His emotions were running rampant, and he was having the time of his life.

Along the way, they saw giraffes. Standing tall and proud, the orange and white titans were truly a sight to behold. It's said that people don't really know how tall giraffes actually are until they see them in person. The same could be said for people, you can't really tell what kind of personality one would be having from a distance.

"Mom! Look! They're so tall!" Ben yelled.

As soon as he did, the jeep driver turned around and gave him a stern look.

"Listen, little boy, this is no place to make noise. Any of these animals can get scared and attack," the man added.

Ben's mother sat him down.

As the safari went along, they saw more and more animals. Rhinos, hippos, crocodiles, cheetahs — the whole lot. The air was thick and dry. Everyone was having to drink water, again and again, just to make sure they didn't choke to death.

After driving for some time, they finally saw it — in all his might and macho, his mane flowing in the wind and his eyes looking across his kingdom — the king of the jungle. The jeeps stopped. At some distance ahead, sitting proud was a lion. Surrounded by his pack of females and cubs, he sat there as the king that he was. His mane was thick and unruly, covering the length of his face and down to his torso. This lion was no ordinary wild cat. This was a true king. This was the lion that people are told the stories of. These are the lions that are the stuff of legends.

The whole group couldn't help but simply stare in sheer awe. They were blown away. It was as if they were seeing some sort of mythical being that had come down from the sky. When the bus driver said that this was going to be a life-changing experience, this was it. Or so they thought. One would assume that at this point, there was nothing else left to see, but as fate would have it, the climax was yet to come.

As they took pictures and made videos of the lion and his pack, the drivers cracked open the fridge and handed everyone a box of juice. Sipping on the chilled sugary juice gave everyone the kick that they needed after being drained on the drive over there. It was no surprise that as fun as this safari was, it was also draining. It was not easy being out in the plains of Africa, especially at a time when the sun was beating down like a dirty orange laser.

After having replenished their reserves, taking all the pictures and videos that they could, it was now time to head back home. It had been several hours since the safari had started, and there was only so much that they were going to be able to see. Resources were limited, and there were also other groups who were waiting for their safaris. This was a busy time of the year, and little time was wasted when it came to these safaris. Nothing was left out, but it was also not something that could be prolonged for no reason.

As the jeeps were getting ready to make a turn, Ben turned around to take a look at the lion one last time. Coincidentally enough, the lion turned his head and looked right at Ben. Feeling as if two souls had been intertwined, Ben was mesmerized by the sheer aura that this lion had. Ben felt like he was changed. He felt like a new person. His love for animals only deepened, and now that he had met eyes with the king of the jungle, there was little left for him to see.

Suddenly, out of nowhere, a bullet tore through the lion's head and blood splashed everywhere. The whole group went numb. The drivers went numb. The security guards stood up in both vehicles.

"Poachers!" The lead officer said.

Ben's parents were gob smacked. They knew what was happening, and what made it worse was that the kids had seen it. These are the kind of things that you hope no one ever sees, especially your little son who is in love with animals. This is the last thing that you want him to see.

Still locked in on the trance, it took Ben a moment to realize that something was wrong. He wasn't ready to come to terms with what happened just yet. He was confused.

"Uhh ... Dad? What's happening? What happened to the lion?"

"Son! It'll all be okay. The lion will be okay. Don't worry!" He consoled. Knowing that your son's heart was about to shatter was a kick to the gut. To make matters worse, knowing that there was nothing you can do about it was just a whole other level of pain.

Through the trees, a group of men dressed in vests and cargo pants emerged. They had bandanas across their heads and scarves across their faces. These were the damned poachers that the park was protecting these animals from, and there was still some way that they had gotten in.

Knowing that something was wrong, the lionesses made a run for it. They knew that they were next, so they darted away before they could be hunted. Lying there, lifeless, and in a pool of his own blood, was the king. The once-mighty beast that had been ruling over his territory for years was now no more. It was an unfitting end to what must have been a magnificent life. To be gunned down as a result of the greed of others is truly something that no king wishes to face.

When it dawned on Ben that the lion was dead, he was disconsolate. He was in a flurry of tears and beyond himself. He was unable to hold in the emotions that came along with this and he was bawling his eyes out.

The guards jumped out of the car and began yelling at the poachers. Hearing them, the poachers made a run for it, disappearing into the bush from where they had emerged.

***

Ever since Ben got back to the hotel from the safari, he was silent. His mom had seen him crying quietly. He wasn't eating or drinking anything. He didn't even go to the pool, although he loved swimming. When she couldn't see her son hurting like that anymore, Mary held Ben by the shoulders and took him to her room. Her husband and the rest of the kids were not around, so they had some privacy.

She sat Ben down on the bed and said, "Honey, what's wrong?"

Her kind words and sympathetic voice were perhaps the last straw. Ben started to cry his eyes out.

"Mom ... mom..." he sputtered.

"I'm here, honey," Mary said, rubbing Ben's back. She had tears in her eyes, too, but she held them back. She had to stay strong for Ben.

"They killed the lion," Ben said, wiping his face with his arm, but fresh tears still ran down his face.

"I know," Mary whispered. She couldn't lie to her son anymore and tell him that everything was okay. She had realized Ben had learned of the cruelties of the world. He had, in fact, become an eyewitness to it. It was better to come clean and tell him what had really happened. "They did kill him, Honey. And it was a mean, mean, cruel thing to do."

Ben hiccupped and cried some more while Mary held him close.

"But we shouldn't treat animals this way, mom," Ben said.

"You're right, baby. You're absolutely right."

"I am never going to forgive that man," Ben declared.

His mom just rubbed his back and nodded.

In his heart, Ben had made a decision: *I will avenge the death of that lion and every other majestic animal that's been killed so cruelly by these madmen. I will get them the justice they deserve!*

Chapter 3: The Veterinarian

Time heals all wounds, or so they say. There are many stories, movies, songs, and art pieces that represent that notion. Many people have told their stories and relegated their experiences about how time was all it took for their wounds to heal. No matter how gaping or deep those wounds might be, a lot of people say that they healed with time. However, wounds can be pretty tricky.

When we get hurt or suffer an injury, our perspective changes in a slight manner. For instance, if you happen to suffer a slight burn, then from that point onward, you might become a little more cautious around the fire or things that are too hot. It may not last permanently, and it may not even be that intense, but there is a significant impact on your psyche.

Some injuries tend to leave a permanent mark though. It may not even be slight or temporary. Some wounds tend to be so deep that they tear through bone and tissue. They reach inside you till they have touched your heart. These wounds can take a lifetime to heal, or they may not heal even then. A lot of people suffer from trauma and experiences that leave them with such wounds. They cannot leave behind scars that are always going to remind them of what happened and how it happened.

Going through life, we often overlook slight injuries or grievances. We brush past them because our skin has thickened over time and we have grown up learning to live with such minor inconveniences. We act like it didn't even happen.

However, it is not until we suffer through some huge scars that we are reminded of how much it can hurt. Of how our pain threshold has not increased but only numbed over time. That is how some wounds work. They take us by surprise and the shock of the hurt is sometimes more impactful than the injury itself.

There are many different kinds of pain and trauma a person can go through in life. Human beings are often perceived as weak and fragile creatures, but that is not true. Humans are very strong and resilient. We go through our lives suffering multiple injuries and wounds, not only physically but also spiritually. We suffer the pain of varying degrees throughout our lifetime, suffering through silence or crying out loud. We get hurt over and over again, sometimes even in the same spot. Yet, humans continue to carry on living as if nothing ever happened.

We continue to laugh, cry, love, and live through every experience that makes up a fulfilling life. We fall in love over and over again, even after getting betrayed or having our hearts broken. We continue to look for success or accomplishing new things, even after failing at some. We keep working toward a happier life, even after living through some really difficult and painful times. Human beings are resilient to the point of it being a fatal flaw. Some might think it is our tendency to heal quickly or over time that helps us be so strong. However, it is the fact that we refuse to give up hope for a better life and world that makes us so readily available to get hurt again and again. It is simply because we believe that it will get better, things will improve, and happiness will find us. In conclusion, time may be able to heal some wounds. Ben never believed in that notion though. He knew some wounds never heal, no matter how much time passes by, and he himself was living proof of that. He had lived a simple yet unproblematic life, as some people would say. He had loving parents who made sure he was provided for and had a good life. They treated him with adoration, and he never had any problems growing up. He also had a good relationship with his siblings, so there weren't any problems there either. All in all, Ben had a good life — nothing that he could or wanted to complain about.

Ben was always a go-getter, not too obsessive, but when he set his mind to something, he would do whatever was needed to achieve it. That was a philosophy he applied to everything in his life. When he was in school, he had decided that he wanted to be a source of comfort for the poor, helpless animals. He felt self-pity for all these animals who didn't have anyone to care for them. . He wanted to be a veterinarian. He became passionate about it and did everything he could to become one. When he graduated with his DVM degree, he felt a sense of accomplishment he had never felt before. He knew he was on the right path.

Never once did Ben ever look back from that day onward. He set on the path to take care of and help animals and never had doubts about it. His family and friends were proud of him, supporting his choice of career wholeheartedly, because why would anyone not? Ben grew up knowing that it was all he wanted to do — help animals. He wanted to be the voice they didn't have and help them get the rights they deserved. That was why Ben was also involved in charity and animal rights activities. He wanted to play his part and do it well.

As a whole, Ben never had many struggles or problems in life. Nothing too dramatic or hard, at least. To everyone, his life seemed simple and sorted out. There were times when Dylan even commented on it.

"Man, I envy you so much sometimes. You never have to worry about anything in life. I wish I had a simple life like yours," he once said to Ben.

Ben knew it and acknowledged that fact. But he was also human and had his own share of problems as well. He just didn't like sharing them with the world. As he grew up, he had become much more private. It wasn't because of anything major, but just a consequence of growing up. He rarely talked to a lot of people about things that were really bothering him. If it got too much, he would confide in his best friend, Dylan, and that was it. He never understood why he would need to air his issues for the whole world to see.

Growing up also meant that Ben had changed a lot physically. Baby fat gave way to chiseled features. His features didn't change much, except that he grew into them. He had started to resemble his father more and more every day, an observation his mother liked to make very often. Ben knew he was a good-looking man. He could feel the stares of people looking at him appreciatively. He had also gotten quite a lot of attention from girls in college, but he was never really interested in any of that. Dating or relationships were not on his mind. He had a goal in mind and was set on achieving it. Now that he was a vet, with his own clinic and an established career, he still was not interested in dating or enhancing his love life. He may have accomplished his goal of becoming a vet, but he still had many other things he wanted to do further. Relationships were the last thing on his mind. During the years in college and after graduating, he had had a few flings here and there, but none to write home about. He had been so busy with his goals and then his burgeoning career that he paid little attention to the women who had waited around for him. Eventually, when they all left, Ben did not even feel devastated over the loss.

As Ben got ready for work that morning, he stopped to look at himself in the mirror. Yes, there were many things he wanted to accomplish, and none of them was easy or quick. He had to work hard and for a long time to even come close to achieving those goals. Every day he woke up and reminded himself why he was doing what he was doing and where he was headed. He wanted to remain focused on what mattered, not allowing for distractions to lead him astray.

Before he left the apartment, he grabbed his keys, wallet, and watch from the bedside table. He stopped for a second to admire the framed photograph from that safari trip all those years ago. In the picture, his whole family was there. They all seemed happy and carefree, yet there was Ben, standing in the corner, looking far off into the distance, with a somber look on his face. His eyes held questions that the world had no answers for to this day. This picture was what he looked at every day. It reminded him of who he was and what he was working for.

***

"Good morning, Kelly. Morning, Jacob," Ben greeted the receptionist and the trainee who worked in his clinic as he walked in.

"Good morning, Ben!" they chorused.

Ben had asked everyone who worked with him to call him by his first name. This clinic was like his second home, and he considered these people an almost second family of sorts.

Greeting the rest of his staff with a smile, he entered his office, only to be stopped short by the sight of an angry young woman slamming her fists on his desk.

"What the hell is wrong with you, you dumb piece of technology?!" The angry young woman yelled at Ben's printer, glaring at it as if it had personally offended her somehow.

"Um, good morning to you too, Jill," Ben greeted, slightly tentative, yet amused. "What did the printer do to you now?"

Jill was his IT genius who worked magic on the entire clinic's computers and devices. She was quite possibly the smartest person Ben knew. He had hired her within an hour of interviewing her, seeing how intelligent and quirky she was. However, for some mystic reason, the printer and Jill were always in a standoff. Even her high technological skills couldn't keep the printer from ticking her off.

Jill looked up at Ben, her tousled blonde hair getting in her face and obstructing her view of her boss.

"Oh, um," Jill chuckled nervously. "Good morning, doc. I was just..."

"Just having another battle with my poor, old printer?" Ben supplied, amused.

"There is something seriously wrong with it! I am not making this up!" Jill let out, frustrated beyond belief.

"You just had it tuned, and it is working just fine, Jill," Ben reassured.

"No! It's absolutely demonic! It never works for me! Stupid little fu-," Jill immediately stopped herself from cursing, looking up at Ben sheepishly.

Ben loved amusing Jill with her quirky behavior, but one thing he did not allow in his clinic was cursing. After he helped Jill out with the "demonic printer who clearly had it out for her," he settled down to start his day of work. Kelly had placed his organized schedule for the day on his desk as well as had it marked on the planner on his computer. She was nothing if not thorough. As he went through his schedule for the day, he realized he had surgery, a couple of sick pets coming in, regular check-up visits for young animals, etc.

In an hour, Ben received his first patient, a young terrier who had gall bladder issues that needed to be operated on. After taking his vitals, checking him out for any unusual lumps, Jacob went to take his blood work and prep him for the surgery. Ben had seen the terrier named Roger for five years now, ever since he was just a little pup. He had prepared for the surgery as much as possible the night before, hoping the dog would get through surgery without any major issues.

Operating on animals was one of the things that Ben never got used to. It wasn't that he couldn't do it. He had graduated with honors, after all. He was lucky that he had the ability to just switch off everything else but the part of his brain that knew what to do and how to make the animal's suffering stop. Of course, his patients' owners would often ask him how he did it, but he honestly didn't know what to tell them.

After the surgery, Ben saw some of his regular patients that had come in for usual vaccinations and shots. As the day passed in a slow grind, lunchtime came around. Then it was back to seeing people come in with injured and sick pets throughout the day. He had an appointment to see a pair of kittens that were newly adopted and needed to be vaccinated. As a reward and way of saying "thank you", a little girl, Ashley, asked the doctor to name one of the kittens, too.

"I will be honored to name your new friend Ashley," Ben smiled at the little girl.

One of the kittens was completely black, while the other was entirely white. He named the black one "Oreo," which gave Ashley the funny idea to name the white one "Cream."

However, their regular day turned into a dramatic one when a woman came in with her yellow Labrador, unconscious in her arms.

"Please! Help! Help my Bernie! He's hurt!"

The medical staff immediately sprang into action upon seeing the bloody, unconscious dog.

"What happened?" Ben was in emergency mode, hurriedly asking the girl to explain the situation.

"He got hit by a car. I went to take out the trash and didn't know my boyfriend had let him loose. He suddenly ran out into the street, and an oncoming Lexus hit him. Please, help him, doctor!" The girl was in tears, her skin had gotten pale, she was so worried about her dog. Upon looking at her condition the staff immediately started working on saving the dog.

When Ben saw the wound on his head, he knew Bernie was in grave danger.

"What's your name?" Ben asked.

"Katrina."

"Okay, Katrina, I need you to calm down and listen to me. My name is Dr. Ben, and I'm going to try to do everything I can to save Bernie, but you have to answer my questions. Did he immediately go unconscious after getting hit or after a little while? Were his limbs moving? Did he have a seizure on your way over here?"

As Ben fired question after question while still working on Bernie's wounds, Katrina looked anything but calm. She looked terrified. After giving the answers Ben required, they asked her to step outside the operating room and wait for them to give her an update. Ben knew it was severe, but he thought he could still save Bernie.

A long, painstaking hour passed, and Katrina paced impatiently in the waiting room, waiting to hear about Bernie.

"Katrina," Ben called out as he came outside to see her.

"Doctor!" Katrina rushed over to him quickly. "Please tell me he's okay! Please tell me my Bernie's okay!"

Seeing Katrina's tears and desperate condition broke his heart, but he was glad to be the bearer of good news.

"He is absolutely fine. Just a little worse for the wear. He's still unconscious, but he's out of any danger now. His injuries would take at least a month to heal, but he will be fine," Ben announced.

Katrina started sobbing and hugged Ben, surprising him. He wasn't a stranger to his clients showing such gratitude after he saved or treated their pets, but it still surprised him.

"Thank you so much! I am so grateful!" Katrina cried softly, letting the doctor go.

"Yes, well, I am glad you brought him here in time. Now, you're going to have to let him stay here for the night so we can observe him and make sure his head injury doesn't get worse. Then you can take him home tomorrow. Just make sure to redress his wounds regularly and keep him from doing anything strenuous or too exciting," Ben explained to the distraught girl.

Katrina went home a while later, after saying her numerous thanks to everyone over and over again.

"Man, that never gets old," Jill said, as they were winding down for the day. The rest of the staff had already left by then, seemingly relieved after such a hectic ending of the day. "I never get tired of seeing you save the day like that, doc."

Ben sat at his desk, observing the appointment list for the next day. "Hmm, yes. It's always a good day when no patient of mine dies on the operating table."

"You really care a lot about them, don't you?" Jill leaned forward and asked.

"I do. I've always had a connection with animals," Ben said, cracking his knuckles as he leaned back in his leather chair.

"How does it feel to save a life? A life so innocent?" Jill asked curiously.

"It feels like I am doing something important. Like I am doing something that needed to be done," Ben said simply.

"And when it doesn't go well?" Jill asked in a low voice.

"Of course, there are days when not everyone survives. Those are the hardest. It feels like I failed them. Failed on the oath I took to try to save every life I could," Ben muttered while looking away. He had a somber look on his face, much like the young Ben wore in the photograph on his nightstand.

"At least, you know you tried, doc. That's what's important," Jill said sympathetically.

"Yes, I am trying...," Ben murmured.

"Anyways," Jill stood up, grabbing her things and making a move to leave. "I am going to head out now. Good night, doc. See ya tomorrow."

"See you in the morning, Jill. Have a good night," he replied as she left his office.

Only a few minutes later, Ben locked up the clinic and left, too. As he headed home, he thought about how he felt relieved to save Bernie. It might not have been like that for other doctors and vets, but for Ben, every patient counted. He never forgot any one of them, especially cases like Bernie. They were the reason why he was doing what he was doing. They were his purpose.

As Ben reached home and put away his things, instead of heading upstairs to shower and change out of his work clothes, he headed to the back of the house. There was an itch under his skin, an itch that wouldn't be satisfied until he saw it. Padding barefoot on the carpeted floor, he unlocked a room at the back of his house that nobody but him visited, even that was very rare though. No one but him knew what was inside this secret room.

When Ben stepped inside and switched on the light, the room revealed his deepest secret. The walls were covered with newspaper clippings, post-it notes, photographs, etc. It looked like a police officer's investigation room. There were papers and boxes everywhere. As he stepped toward the lone table in the room, covered with even more papers and files, he looked around at what was his true purpose in life. The one thing he never shared with anyone. His passion in life.

He stood in the center and looked at the picture right in the center of the wall. The same picture he had on his nightstand. On its right was a picture of a beautiful golden lion. It was a lot like the lion he had seen being hunted and killed all those years ago. Then on the left of the picture of his family was a simple page torn from his notepad. On the paper was a list of scribbled names of some strangers. Or at least they were strangers to others, but not to Ben. He knew these names like the back of his hand. He had memorized them and could recite them in his sleep. The names were not popular or held any meaning in the outside world.

However, these names were the names of illegal poachers whom Ben had discovered. The list was what kept Ben working so hard toward his goal. He worked and exhausted himself in his search for these illegal poachers who loved harming innocent animals and benefitting from it in illegal and horrible ways. Ben wanted to put a stop to it all. He traced the names on the list, stopping on the one at the top.

Peter

That was the same man who had killed the lion when Ben was a young kid. The same man who had been haunting his dreams. The same man who represented everything Ben hated in the world. He was the one who had to pay. Ben would start with him and slowly make his way down the list. He had to put a stop to it. That was his one true purpose.

There was no one rallying for those poor creatures who were being treated like toys. It was time humanity learned to acknowledge its wrongs and fix them. Ben would do what no one was willing to do. It didn't matter if it was next to impossible or tough as a nail. Ben would accomplish his goals. He would end the horrifying nightmare that he had witnessed and would start with this man.

Chapter 4: King Poacher

Ben had been working against poachers for so long now that he had amassed quite a lot of information against them all. He had done his research and was always collecting new tidbits regarding the people on his list. He might have been after Peter his whole life, but that didn't mean that he didn't keep an eye on all other poachers in the world. His fight's main purpose was not to punish Peter only but every other person who believed in the evil act of poaching. His life was about saving the poor animals who had to deal with humans like Peter, not just Peter.

Once, when Ben was a teen in high school, he went through something horrible. After his AP Biology class, he had a free period. He decided to go outside and enjoy the sun and the fresh air in the schoolyard. When he got outside, he didn't see anyone else around, so he assumed he was alone. It was one of the rare times when he found a moment of quiet and peace around his school. Otherwise, it was always loud and chaotic as high schools are, he supposed.

Ben sat on the warm grass, getting some much-needed sunlight. He liked to keep to himself most of the time and enjoyed spending time with nature. His mother always worried because he was not as social or popular with the kids as she would've liked. Ben knew that his mother worried for no reason. Things always turn out better than you think, sometimes even exceeding your expectations. That's what he liked to believe, at least.

Suddenly, Ben heard muffled laughter from nearby. He swiveled his head around, trying to find the source of the sound. He looked this way and that but could not find anyone. He shrugged it off and went back to his meditative state. However, before he could close his eyes, he heard the laughter again, but this time it was closer and clearer. There was definitely someone nearby. Ben quickly turned to look and saw what he feared the most. Or at least, what 15-year-old Ben feared the most. His bullies.

Ben could see Bart and his group of friends coming closer. For a minute, his heart picked up the pace, and he could feel the sweat roll down his back. He tried to find a way to hide, but he was out in the open, and there was no tree or bush big enough that he could've used as cover. Soon enough, Bart and his friends noticed Ben, and Ben's heart stuttered. The boys had always made life hell for him when they would run into each other in the school hallways, but now Ben was all alone. He was in a quiet place, and nobody would even hear his screams. He gulped.

Bart made his way closer to Ben with a smirk on his face. Ben felt the fear in his heart intensify and shuffled on the grass. He stood up just as Bart made his way over.

"Sup, loser. What are you doin' out here, all alone?" Bart asked.

"I-I-I was just ... I was just...," Ben cursed his stutter internally.

Bobby and his friends laughed.

"You were just...?" Bart inquired.

"It's my free period, so....," Ben said nervously. He really didn't want to get into any trouble that day.

"Free period, huh? Wanna hang out with us then?" Bart asked.

His friends all turned to look at him in shock, not expecting him to ask Ben, of all people, to hang out with them.

"What?" Ben was shocked as well.

"Wanna hang with us?" Bart asked again.

Ben was immediately suspicious. "Is this a trap? Are you gonna take me in the back and beat me up or something?"

Bart laughed heartily and then shook his head, "No, bud. I just wanna show you some slugs we found. You're into that weird shit, right?"

"If by 'weird shit' you mean animals, then, yes. But why?" Ben was confused as to why Bart was being so nice to him all of a sudden.

"Cuz I don't know anyone else who might be able to help me," Bart said simply.

"Yo, Bart, what the hell?" One of Bart's friends asked him.

"Shut up, Mark," Bart rolled his eyes. "So, are you coming or what?"

Ben could feel his head spin. Was he in the twilight zone or something? What was happening?

"If you wanna come with us, then come. If not, then your call," Bart said impatiently.

Ben weighed his options. He wanted to say 'no' so bad, but Bart mentioned slugs. If anything, Ben knew that a boy like Bart shouldn't even go anywhere near slugs. So, maybe it was necessary for Ben to go with Bart just to make sure he didn't hurt any poor slugs. He just hoped that he wouldn't regret his choice later after the boys left him bruised and bloodied in some ditch somewhere.

"Okay, show me the slugs," Ben said, squaring his shoulders. He would at least try to fight them off.

Bart looked surprised. He raised his eyebrows, truly shocked that Ben would say yes. Then he nodded and started leading the way. Ben followed the boys, his heart racing and palms sweating nervously. He knew he could be walking into a trap, but the slugs....

"It's right behind that shed. Do you know it?" Bart mentioned as he kept on walking.

Ben noticed that they were headed to the old shed far behind the school. He swallowed with hesitation but didn't slow down his pace. "Yeah, I've seen it."

"Cool," Bart responded.

Bart's friends kept sharing confused glances with each other. Ben figured that if even his friends didn't know about it, then it couldn't mean that Bart had some nefarious plans under his sleeve, right?

Soon, they came near the shed. It was barely even standing anymore, with its rotting wood and structure that was falling apart. It looked dangerous to enter as if it could fall on anyone who slightly stepped inside. For one minute, Ben had a crazy thought of his parents finding his body in that shed. He shook off the negative and dreadful thoughts, pausing right beside Bart. He walked to the side of the shed, crouching down and reaching out into the mud that was covered with moss and leaves.

"Here they are," Bart picked up a slug and showed it to Ben.

Ben was amazed. Not because he had never seen slugs before, but because he really hadn't been expecting Bart to be telling the truth. Ben took the slug from his hand carefully, feeling its slimy texture tickling his palm. He brought it up to his face to examine.

"Hey, little guy," Ben whispered to it.

Bart laughed and said, "You're talking to it? You're so weird!"

Ben sighed and put the slug back on the ground.

"Yes, Bart, I talk to them. You know, they are living breathing creatures like us, right?"

Bart scowled at Ben's sarcasm and said, "Watch it."

Ben shut up and went to watch the slugs. Bart went behind him, and before Ben could even realize what had happened, he was pushed to the ground—right on top of the slugs. Bart and his friends started laughing like hyenas instantly, pointing at

Ben. Ben was horrified and immediately tried to get up. He gasped and struggled to get up out of the mud. Bart and his friends kept laughing at him, but Ben only thought about the slugs. As soon as he could get up, he sat up and turned to check on the slugs. Tears filled his eyes as he saw what his fall had done to some of them.

Ben turned around to face Bart and his gang of bullies, "You monsters! Look what you have done!"

Bart found a way to control his laughter and replied, "What? They're just slugs."

Ben was horrified. He couldn't believe that someone could be that heartless. How could Bart not think about the slugs? How could he not be affected?

"How can you be so heartless?" Ben whispered with tears in his eyes.

Bart shrugged, and they all laughed again. Soon, they heard the school bell ring in the distance. Bart and his friends ran like bats were after them. Ben just sat there, emotionally wrecked, over the slugs. He kept looking at them and cried. That was the day when he realized that bullies existed in all ages and sizes. It didn't matter how old he got, people like Peter and Bart existed everywhere. They would always find a way to act on their evil intentions. That is why Ben decided to go after them all, not just Peter. He knew that going after Peter was just a start. After him, there were many others just like him he had to take care of.

Peter was the hardest one to crack, though. There wasn't a lot of information about him. Ben had to go to great lengths to collect whatever he could find about the mysterious man. He exhausted all of his resources and talked to everyone he could just to find out the tiniest bit of detail about Peter. However, his hard work had paid off, and he had gathered enough information to know who the man was. Peter was the king poacher, but obviously, he didn't start out that way.

Peter was born in the Czech Republic, but his family had soon migrated to the United States When he was little, he made friends with some Polish kids because they were the closest to his home country and no American kid wanted to be friends with him. The three Polish brothers and Peter grew up normally enough, but when they were in their teens, they witnessed a cockfight.

Cockfights are illegal, but they managed to sneak in. The group was always looking for an adrenaline rush and exciting things to do. Soon enough, they got into the habit of placing bets in cockfights. They would win some and lose some, but it didn't matter—not then, at least—until Peter started winning more than the Polish brothers. Peter had learned how to deduct who would win the fight. They concocted a plan to use Peter's tactics to win even more money. Fast forward a few years, by the time they were in their twenties, they had their own illegal cockfight ring set up.

The business was going well, too well actually, and that got some attention from the authorities. The authorities instructed them to shut down their business. After their illegal side business got shut down, the men were itching to do something even bigger. Instead of the experience scaring them off forever, they were determined to do something even better and more efficient so that they never get caught again. Peter was smart, and so he started researching things that they could do and fly under the radar. When he came across the poaching industry, he wasn't too sure about it at first. It needed a lot of money to be set up and to pay off people so they could get away scot-free.

A year or so later, he was approached by a millionaire who had been observing him during his cockfight ring days. The millionaire promised to finance his next venture as long as he did it alone. Peter saw the dollar signs and was already sold. He told the Polish brothers that he was striking it alone— something that didn't sit well with them, but they couldn't stop him. After striking a deal with the millionaire, Peter was on his way to becoming an illegal poacher.

Some might think Peter didn't like animals, with the way he was involved in such activities, while the truth was that he loved animals. He thought they were beautiful, majestic creatures of nature. His mentality was that animals were amazing and could be even more so if they were used for the bounties they had to offer. He saw them as something God-given to humans to use, because why would something be so beautiful and not be used?

Ben had learned all of this and more, horrified to his core. He didn't know whether to admire Peter's cunning ways or be disgusted by his lack of conscience for other living beings. He was always looking for ways to interrupt Peter's business and make sure he suffered. Yet, he had never gotten a chance to do so because he was still finding it hard to collect all the information.

One day, Ben got a tip. It was a regular day, but he heard through the grapevine that Peter was smuggling one of his shipments that night. The shipment was, of course, that of invaluable items achieved from his illegal poaching business.

Ben could not let this opportunity pass. He decided to take some action and prepared to go interrupt the shipment. He had been ready his whole life to meet Peter again and make sure he got what he deserved. As Ben prepared the things he would take with him, he realized how difficult it would be for him.

The mission was to destroy or interrupt the shipment before it was loaded onto the ship. He still needed to figure out how exactly he would do that and leave unscathed. He packed a bag with night-vision goggles, binoculars, bionic ear equipment, some snacks, a tablet with the information and location loaded, a few explosives, and, of course, his long-range rifle.

Ben didn't like carrying weapons, but for this mission, it was required. How else would he destroy the shipment? Even one destroyed container could cause Peter a lot of damage. As Ben drove his truck to the docks that night, he remembered the day he had witnessed Peter killing that lion. That image never left his mind. He had never forgotten that day and probably never will. That was the only thing that he needed for the motivation to do this.

When he was growing up, Ben always had somewhat of a timid personality. He was active in his studies and extracurricular activities, but nothing more. He definitely didn't like violence. So, for him to grow up and become a vet was very apropos of his character. What other people wouldn't expect is for Ben to pack up explosives, a gun, and some spy equipment to thwart an illegal businessman's operations. Ben knew, however, that he needed to do this. He needed to hurt Peter, and this was the only way now.

As Ben approached the site, he could see that the docks were not as empty, considering how late it was. He parked his truck far away from the big cars he could see on the docks. He sat in his car, quietly waiting. Then he saw some men in dark suits near a cargo container. They were talking among themselves quietly, and in the distance, Ben couldn't hear them properly. He got out his bionic ear and stepped outside the truck as quietly as a mouse. He tiptoed toward the edge of one container and hid. As he turned on the bionic equipment, he could hear scattered pieces of information.

"...inform boss ... shipment containers ... hurry ... buyer's waiting..."

Ben had heard enough. He needed to move now. After the men in suits went away, he saw the opportunity to attack. He crept toward the container they were guarding and took out one of the explosives from his bag. He stuck it on the front of the container, then moved to do the same to the side. Just as he stepped away from the container, he heard the sound of a gun cocking from behind him that made him freeze.

"Hold it," a gruff voice said from behind.

Ben slowly raised his hands in the air and turned around. He was facing five large men in suits, obviously Peter's minions.

They were all armed with angry scowls and guns that were pointing at Ben at that moment. He knew he was in trouble, and he had expected this, but he wasn't totally unprepared.

"You work for Peter, right?" Ben asked the man in front.

"Who the hell are you?" he asked in response.

"I am someone who knows Peter from a long time ago. You can tell him I said, 'Hi,'" Ben said.

"You are about two seconds away from dying. Why don't you tell me what you were doing so I can make it peaceful?" the rough-looking man threatened.

"Well, you see. I am a vet. And I cannot, in good conscience, let you do this. So, I am destroying your container," Ben replied in a nonchalant manner.

The man looked at him, then back at his group, and then they all started laughing. Ben smiled at them as if he was enjoying himself, too. Then, while the men were still laughing, Ben clicked the detonator button that he was hiding inside his palm, and the explosion occurred.

The impact of the explosion threw everyone off and straight onto a hard concrete floor. For a couple of minutes, everything was silent, since Ben could not hear anything. He was disoriented and dizzy for a few minutes.

Ben could feel his ears ringing and his head feeling fuzzy as he tried to get his bearings back. He slowly sat up, his vision blurry, and saw the other men in similar conditions. As he slowly sat up, the dizziness prevailed, but even through his blurry vision, he could see the two destroyed containers he had set the explosives to.

Ben stood up on shaky legs and couldn't help but let out a relieved chuckle at the destruction he had caused. It felt *good*. It wasn't a lot, but he could bet that those two containers alone must have cost Peter at least a few million bucks.

Through his periphery, Ben saw Peter's goons standing up as well and knew that it was time for him to rush before they caught him again. He immediately started running toward his car that was parked a few yards away, quite inconveniently. His legs were still a little shaky and vision compromised from the explosion, but he powered through it.

He was only a few feet away from his truck when the men opened fire. Ben ducked as shots after shots were fired at him, all by the men running and shooting after him. Ben quickened his pace and tried to duck and hide behind the containers as he ran to save his life. He got to his truck's driver's side door but immediately ducked as a bullet whizzed past his head.

He was terrified and immediately jumped into his truck. They started firing at his truck, with one shot going through his windshield as he started the truck. The glass shattered, and Ben tried to save himself as much as he could while revving the engine to get out of there.

A few pieces of glass stuck to his arm, and he winced at the pain, but thankfully his truck's engine started, and he swerved the truck around, dodging the onslaught of bullets, and rushed out of there as the tires squealed on the pavement. He drove faster than he ever had, soon entering the middle of the traffic on the freeway and breathing a sigh of relief. He checked into the rearview mirror to see if anyone was following him, but nothing seemed suspicious.

That night, as Ben got home tired, disoriented, and injured, he knew he couldn't run around like a vigilante again. He needed backup, more surveillance equipment, and a lot better strategy. If he wanted to take Peter down, he had to be smart about it, not reckless. While he stitched up the wounds on his arm on his own, Ben started planning his strategy. As fun as it felt to damage Peter's shipment, Ben had to do a lot more than that to officially end Peter's business. So he started thinking about the exact things he would need to take Peter down once and for all.

He knew that getting Peter's business to shut down needed a much bigger solution. He had to get help from the authorities. However, getting someone like Peter convicted required hard work and effort. Ben knew what Peter did and was pretty sure that even the authorities knew what he did. Yet, getting proof of all of that was more difficult than it seemed. Ben had researched and looked into it for years, but he had never found anything that stuck. The information he was able to gather was all temporary. Ben needed something more concrete so that it could stand in court.

Getting Peter convicted was the piece that would create the domino effect, and the whole poaching business would shut down. He was the head that needed to be cut off. Ben was ready to do whatever it took to take him down and put in as much effort as he needed to. However, he also knew that he couldn't do it alone. He needed at least one person on his side so that he could have support. Ben needed backup and someone he could rely on to help him with his mission.

Collecting evidence would not be hard if he had someone monitoring surveillance for him and guiding him safely throughout the whole thing. His plan depended on the fact that he needed to gather enough incriminating evidence to put Peter behind bars. Yet, he knew his plan would fail if he couldn't get someone to help him through it all.

The only problem was that Ben didn't know anyone he could trust enough to involve them in his plans. He had never told anyone about this secret of his and didn't know if he could tell now. He couldn't tell Dylan either because he didn't think Dylan would approve of his ideas.

The next day at work, Ben was still distracted by his thoughts of who he could recruit to help him with his mission to get Peter convicted. He needed someone who was good with equipment and gadgets, and so someone technologically skilled. They also had to be trustworthy, of course. Then they needed to be someone who was sympathetic to the cause. While he was gazing off in the distance, thinking about his problem, his gaze fell on Jill.

"Jacob, you just have to log out and then log back in. It's really that simple," Jill explained to Jacob while he looked a bit nervous about something.

Ben paused and tilted his head. Jill was a tech genius—the smartest person he knew, actually. She was also someone he trusted. Jill was known to be an animal rights activist as she actively took part in doing her part for them. Ben thought long and hard about it. Jill seemed to be the perfect candidate for his secret job. One question kept ringing around his head, though.

Could Jill be trusted with such a secret and important mission?

Chapter 5: Tech Support

As Ben looked around the café, he finally spotted the familiar face of his best friend, Dylan. They both smiled at each other, and Ben made his way toward the table where Dylan was sitting. The café they were meeting at was a personal favorite of Ben. When Dylan had called him that morning, asking if he was free to hang out at lunchtime, Ben had agreed. He had told him to meet at this spot because he loved to frequent it. The pastel theme, the mismatched antique wooden chairs, the friendly staff, and the familiar smell of coffee surrounded them like a warm blanket.

Ben had first visited this café with his dad. He had had a bad day after getting rejected in baseball tryouts for a second year in middle school. He was disappointed because he thought his dad was disappointed in him. Even though he was good at extracurricular activities, he was never much of an athlete. He knew how much his dad wanted him to be part of the school's baseball team. His dad had taken him to this café after school and bought him a milkshake with extra whipped cream. It was his favorite. That day, his dad had said something to him that had stuck with him forever.

"Son, no matter what you do, always follow your heart. It doesn't matter if the whole world is against you or doesn't care about the things you do. If it's important to you, then it should be the most important thing in the world to you."

At the time, little Ben didn't know how much he would cherish those words during later years of his life. When he got accepted into veterinarian school, he remembered those words. When he graduated and then got his license, he remembered those words. And when he went after Peter that night at the docks, he remembered those words again.

This café had a little soft spot in Ben's heart, which is why he preferred coming there for coffee, light lunches, and just to unwind after a hard day at work. As he took his seat and greeted his best friend, he finally relaxed.

"Hard day?" Dylan asked, noticing Ben's stiff posture and tense muscles.

"You could say that; yeah. Had to put down a young Labrador today. His family was devastated," Ben recounted sadly.

No matter how much he studied for this and how many times he performed treatments like that, it never got easy for Ben. His love and sympathy for animals made it hard for him sometimes, but he was still a great veterinarian, so he used his empathy to comfort the family of those innocent lives.

After placing their orders, they caught up a little on each other's lives and days. While the coffee arrived, Dylan took out his phone and answered a few texts and DMs on social media. Scrolling through Twitter, he saw the local news feed.

"Oh man, did you hear about the explosion at the docks the other day?" Dylan threw out while still scrolling on his phone.

Ben stayed silent for a few seconds, not knowing how to respond to that.

"They think it could've been a gang activity," Dylan said casually, not noticing how Ben was starting to look more than a little nervous.

"Really? That's ... bad," Ben said, chastising himself for such a lame response.

"Yeah, it was," Dylan put away his phone and turned his attention back on Ben. "So, how are things with you really?"

"Things are ... okay. For the most part," Ben responded. He still hadn't decided if he should finally confide in Dylan regarding his plans for Peter.

Dylan had always been supportive and had encouraged him through every endeavor in life, but this one was a little too risky. Ben wasn't sure if Dylan would agree with his methods or even his ideas.

"Are you sure?" Dylan inquired.

"Yes! Of course. Why are you so concerned?" Ben said laughingly.

"Because all you do is go to that clinic of yours and hold yourself up in your house with that friend of yours, Silice," Dylan listed off, looking as if he was counting the seven deadly sins and not Ben's usual routine.

"And what's wrong with that? I'm career-driven, introverted, and quiet, and I like staying at home with a book or a journal to relax," Ben said with a shrug.

"You seriously don't see any problems with that?" Dylan's eyebrows were raised up to his hairline.

Ben just gave him a blank look in return.

"What about friends? Socializing? Going out? Having fun? Dating? All that stuff that normal people do to enjoy their lives, y'know...," Dylan said, looking at Ben incredulously.

"Why are you so surprised? I was always like this," Ben was amused more than anything.

"Because! You're my best friend! And I feel like I am failing you if I don't help you enjoy your life at least once in a while," Dylan looked sad.

"Hey, it's okay. You've always looked out for me, Dylan. And I appreciate it so much. But, parties, going out, and all that stuff is just ... not me. You know I am more comfortable staying home or being in my clinic," Ben assured his friend.

It was true. Dylan had never once abandoned or left Ben out, not even when they were in college. Dylan was an outgoing extrovert who loved having fun and partying. Yet, he had never left Ben just to go have fun. He would always bring him along and spend time with him. Dylan and Ben might have been complete opposites, but it was what made their friendship so great.

They could fill out each other's blank spaces. Dylan had helped Ben get out of his shell and have fun when all he wanted to do was study. Dylan was the one who had helped him get his first girlfriend. Dylan was his best friend, and without him, Ben didn't know how much worse off he'd be.

In order to cheer him up, Ben started recounting old tales of the parties he had gone to with Dylan when they were young. It worked, and in no time, the two were laughing about silly things they did when they got stupidly drunk. Rather, when Dylan got stupidly drunk, and Ben would go along with it.

Ben was right. Hanging out with Dylan was just what he needed to forget about the hard day at work and recover. Dylan even asked about Silice, Ben's little, black-and-white Border Collie. He was in close competition of being Ben's best friend. Dylan didn't mind, though, because he loved the little, furry brat. They had such a funny relationship. At times, Silice almost seemed a little jealous of Dylan, but then they would also play together the most.

After a day of hanging out and just being his normal self with his best friend, Ben knew it was time to get back to work. Just as the thought popped into his head, he got a text notification on his phone. He pulled it out and read the text sent by Jacob. There was a client waiting for him with a new patient who he needed to look at.

"Dylan, I have a patient at the clinic. I'm so sorry, but I'm going to have to rush," Ben said apologetically.

"Oh, no, it's alright. You have your duties. We had fun, though," Dylan said with a smile.

"Yeah," Ben was genuine. He needed the lighthearted banter and funny conversations with Dylan after everything that had happened in the past couple of weeks.

The two friends hugged and said their goodbyes. Dylan left, and Ben was on his way out after collecting his things. Arriving back at the clinic, he parked his car in the reserved spot and got out. He never liked making any patient wait because he knew it could be dangerous. He was rushing to enter the clinic, which was why he didn't really see where he was going and ended up stumbling into a woman. He cursed under his breath as his bag fell to the pavement and some documents came pouring out since he had never zipped his bag closed. That ought to teach him a lesson.

Trying to collect his things from the pavement quickly, he was suddenly joined by a pair of other hands. The woman was apologizing and helping him collect his things while Ben still refused to look in her direction. It wasn't on purpose. He just wanted to hurry.

"Hey, I really am sorry. I didn't mean to make you drop your things," the woman said, sounding upset and a bit confused about how Ben was acting.

Ben finally looked up in exasperation and paused. The woman was a beautiful brunette who looked way too out of place in that parking spot. She was wearing a deep-emerald-green wrap dress, her hair was pin-straight, and her makeup looked natural and light. On her feet were beige stilettos. Ben gave her a once-over and wondered what this woman would be doing in the parking lot of his clinic. She wasn't even holding a pet.

"You know, I've apologized to you multiple times now, and you still refuse to acknowledge it," the woman said with a bemused expression on her pretty face.

Yes, Ben could acknowledge a pretty woman. He wasn't blind. "It's okay. I'm sorry, actually. I was in a rush; I have a patient waiting for me inside...," he said by way of explanation.

"Wait," the woman looked a bit shocked. "You're Dr. Ben? The vet?"

Ben frowned in confusion, "Yes?" It made it sound like he was unsure of his own identity.

"Oh my god," the woman muttered with wide eyes.

Ben was even more confused. Why was she acting like she knew him?

"I've been looking for you!" She explained.

"Looking for me? What? Why?" Ben was so lost.

"Right. Sorry. I should start from the beginning," the girl chuckled nervously. "My name is Dana Harper. I am a reporter for the City Report."

"City Report? Well, how do you know me then, Ms. Harper?" Ben asked inquisitively.

"I was told to do a piece on the recent animal rights protest that was held in the city square. I was digging through a few records, and I noticed you are always at the forefront of all these animal rights activities. I thought meeting you and maybe doing an interview with you would give me a great angle for my piece," Dana explained with a smile.

"You wanna interview me? For a paper?" Ben inquired. He was tired of looking confused, but he couldn't help it.

"Yes! You're one of the most active members who's also quite a prominent member of the community. I mean, I've only ever heard great things about you, Dr. Ben," Dana said.

Ben didn't know how to respond to that. An interview seemed like bragging about things that he didn't want to brag about. He was only doing what he thought was right, and he wasn't the only one. He was a bit torn, and then he remembered why he was rushing in the first place. He quickly checked his watch and noticed he was late.

"Shit," Ben cursed under his breath again. "Um, Ms. Dana, I have a patient waiting inside, and I really have to go now."

"Oh, really? Damn, I wish we could've continued this conversation some more," Dana expressed sadly.

Ben hesitated for a little, knowing that he had to go inside quickly, but he also wanted to see what Dana was talking about.

"Um, how about this? If you have time, can you wait around? Then we can chat after I'm done dealing with this patient, unless you have somewhere to be," Ben proposed.

"I have a meeting to get to, but maybe I could catch you some other time," Dana said with a smile.

Ben nodded, and they said their goodbyes. He rushed inside the clinic, and Jacob asked him where he had been. The patient needed emergency attention, and Ben felt bad that he had gotten so late.

***

A couple of days after that encounter with the reporter, Ben was in his office. It was past his time to go home, and he hadn't even realized. When he happened to glance at the clock, he felt his eyes widen in shock.

"What? How did it get so late?" He asked no one in particular.

"You tell me, doc," came Jill's voice as she entered his office.

"Jill? What are you doing here? Why haven't you gone home?" Ben asked her.

"I was going to, but then I noticed your weird mood and how you didn't seem to want to leave," Jill said. "I guess I didn't want to leave you alone when you looked so ... lost."

"It's nothing, Jill," Ben gave her a small smile. "I was just thinking about some stuff."

He was thinking about Peter and how he was still continuing to reign his terror on wildlife around the world. Ben was still working to gather evidence against him, but he had failed miserably. It was worse than when he tried to find information on the man himself. He had dug as deep as he could, yet his efforts had failed him. The frustration and hopelessness of the situation were starting to get to him, hence the reason he missed the time to go home.

77

"Listen, Ben," Jill said, a bit reluctant. "If there's something going on with you ... some issue you're having ... I am here to listen if you want to talk."

Ben smiled at Jill's sweetness, "You're really one of a kind of an employee, aren't you?"

"I try to be," Jill quipped with a smile.

Ben was about to tell her not to worry about it and have a good night, but then he paused. Hadn't he discovered that maybe Jill was the right kind of person to help him with his plans? She was a genius with tech and was a good employee of his. He might even say that they were friends. He had given it thought the night he attacked Peter's shipment, but after that, he had never thought about it again. Until now, that is. He looked at Jill and analyzed her again. She was a bit quirky, quite cheerful, and always taking care of the people in the clinic. She was a real gem of an employee, and Ben thought maybe it couldn't hurt to test his theory out. Ben remembered the day she came in for her interview for the position as clear as day.

A bubbly blonde had entered Ben's office, and he was a bit surprised. All the candidates he had interviewed thus far had been different. They definitely didn't carry a phone with a sparkly cover.

"Hi!" The girl bounced over and took a seat in front of Ben's desk. She introduced herself, and Ben found himself endeared by her childlike innocence.

Ben conducted the interview, thinking that maybe the girl just wasn't sure of what she wanted because she didn't look like an IT technician. It's not that she wasn't smart, but rather she didn't act like it. Usually, when people were really intelligent, they would act like they were the smartest person in the room. With the way Jill carried herself, Ben didn't expect to see the resume that she sent.

She had been to MIT and had done many technological courses from various prestigious institutions. She had also been in a high position throughout her academics, proving her genius. Ben was honestly very impressed. More impressed than he had been with the other candidates.

"So, can I just ask you one last thing?" Ben asked her as the interview was wrapping up.

"Of course. That's kind of why I'm here," Jill chuckled.

Ben laughed too.

"Why this job? According to your resume, you are actually overqualified for this position," Ben said, puzzled.

"Well," Jill hesitated and looked down at her hands that were folded in her lap. "Honestly? I like the safety aspect of it."

"Safety?" Ben was even more puzzled.

"See, I have worked in a big corporation before. I was their head of IT, as you can see from my resume. But, a position such as that comes with its set of risks and safety issues. The corporation had to deal with constant threats, as any other corporation does. I had to deal with them myself. My love affair with computers started when I was really young. I liked the idea of everything being at my fingertips. I loved how, with just a few codes, I could create my own thing. My own world," Jill shared.

Ben nodded, understanding what she was talking about.

"But then, working for that company made me realize the dangers involved. I was always a homebody. I never liked going out, and I especially never liked fights or anything violent. So, you can imagine how much it freaked me out when I worked for such a large company and had to deal with literal terrorists," Jill explained.

"Terrorists?!" Ben was shocked.

"You'd be surprised at how much terrorism the technology industry has to face on a daily basis. These companies are at the forefront of the target list of every terrorist group in the world," Jill told Ben.

He was stunned into silence. Then he spoke, "That must have been really hard for you then."

"It was," Jill nodded solemnly. "When someone found my personal accounts and threatened me on them, then that was when I knew I had to get out. I couldn't work in such a hostile environment anymore."

"I understand," Ben said sympathetically.

"That's why, when I saw your ad online, I knew I should apply. I mean, yeah, you don't have the same benefits or salary as that job, but safety is what I need. That's my number-one priority, to stay as far away from violence as possible," Jill said.

"Yeah, a veterinarian clinic is not really the hot spot for terrorists," Ben said humorously.

Jill giggled, "Exactly. What could be safer than a bunch of cute puppies?"

"Oh, you should still be careful, though. Some of the cats we get are ... phew!" Ben responded, joking around with Jill.

They both laughed.

Ben knew then that Jill would be the perfect person for his clinic. Not only because she was so smart and obviously insanely talented but also because of her personality; she was bubbly when Ben was quiet and brooding. She was the positive energy that he needed to surround himself with.

The next morning, Ben called her to confirm her hiring and had to pull his phone away from his ear when Jill started squealing and screaming about how she was 'going to be the most amazing employee' he had ever seen!

Ben knew he had made the right decision then.

Ben smiled, thinking about how he had met Jill and was immediately taken by her. They had become friends after just her first day at the clinic. It surprised him because he never imagined himself being friends with someone like Jill, but there he was. Now, he was about to ask her to become an even closer friend and confidante of his.

"Jill, can I ask you something?" Ben asked.

"Of course!" Jill said immediately and took a seat in front of his desk, eager to listen to what her boss had to say.

"What do you believe in?" he asked simply.

Jill blinked in surprise because she hadn't been expecting that.

"Um, like religion?" She asked with confusion painting her words.

"No. Like lifestyle. What are some of the things you believe in? Morals, ideas, opinions, etc. Things that make you who you are," Ben elaborated.

"Oh," Jill was a bit taken aback by the line of questioning, but she didn't mind. She liked discussing these things with her friends and considered the doctor a friend.

"I think I believe in doing the right thing. I know that sounds cheesy, lame, or whatever, but it's true. I think that every human being has a responsibility to uphold their status as a human. I mean, who are we if we are not empathetic?"

Ben was a little shocked to hear that. He definitely didn't expect that.

"Wow, Jill, I," Ben found himself lost for words. "I'm impressed. Really."

Jill smiled and said, "It's just that I've seen a lot of people in my life who had the power to change things or do something nice for the other person, but they didn't—all because it would disrupt their lives. I vowed to myself never to be like that. I always said that if I was ever in a position to help someone in any way possible, I would. Especially if it is the right thing to do."

Ben gave her a huge smile and said, "You don't even know how happy you've made me with that."

Jill tilted her head in confusion and asked, "What do you mean?"

"I mean that I have something important to share with you," Ben said.

He was ready to trust Jill. It had been like a test, and she had passed with flying colors. He knew he could trust her. His gut had told him so.

"What, like a secret?" Jill said, her eyes wide with glee and looking way too excited.

"Yes, like a secret. A secret you can never tell anyone because it's gravely serious," Ben said, and with his expression, Jill understood the severity of the situation.

Jill nodded and asked, "So, what is it?"

"I can't just tell you. I have to show you," Ben responded.

The two got in the doctor's truck as he drove to his house. Jill was a bit anxious about what the doctor had to show her. She trusted him, but she couldn't figure out what deep, dark secret the doctor could have. When they entered the house, Ben quietly took her to the locked room near the back of the house, and they entered. As he switched on the light, her loud gasp was a reaction he expected afterward.

"Oh my god," Jill muttered. "Ben! What's this?" She turned around to see him with an incredulous look on her face.

Ben just took a seat at the table and got ready to tell her everything. Jill interrupted him, though.

"You're not like a serial killer or something, are you?" Jill asked, not even looking scared.

"Well, if I was, you were incredibly wrong to trust me and follow me to my house without informing anyone," Ben replied. Then he chuckled at the slightly scared expression on Jill's face. "I'm kidding! I'm kidding!"

After Jill calmed down and sat down to hear the explanation, Ben started to tell a tale that he hadn't told anyone. Not in a long time, at least. The last person he told this to was Dylan, and that was years ago. As his long story ended, Jill continued to look at him with wide eyes, her mouth slightly open.

"Is that really true? Did that really happen?" Jill asked, shocked to her core. She knew what poaching was, but to hear the doctor's horrific tale, well, *horrified* her.

"Every word of it," Ben confirmed.

"I'm so sorry you had to go through something like that. Especially at such a young age," Jill expressed with regret.

"It's fine. I've learned how and where to focus my energy," he told her.

"And you really wanna do this? Like, go after some big poaching mafia guy, steal some evidence of his criminal behavior, and then expose him?" Jill inquired with hesitation.

"Yes. I have to bring him to justice. He's gotten away with way too much already," Jill could see how the doctor was trying to keep calm while he said that.

"Okay, but do you realize how dangerous this is? He's literally a gangster. And you're ... you ... you can't even hurt a fly!" Jill thought it was crazy. Justifiable, but crazy.

"Exactly. I can't even hurt a fly, and yet, these monsters are out there hurting so many more animals that it makes me sick. You said it yourself, Jill. You believe in doing the right thing. Is this not the right thing?" Ben said desperately.

"Doc, I completely agree with you. But, it's dangerous. And you're not equipped to take on a criminal gang," Jill was worried.

"I'll be fine. You know why? Because I am recruiting you. You are going to help me stay safe and informed. You can help me get the evidence I need to put that man behind bars like he deserves," Ben stated.

Jill was shocked again. "Me?!"

Ben nodded, "You're one of the smartest people I know. You have the exact skills I need for this mission. I also trust you. I know I can trust you."

"Whoa, doc, that's a whole lot of faith you're putting in me," Jill laughed nervously.

"That's just how it is. So," Ben looked at her with a deep look in his eyes.

Jill had never seen the calm and collected doctor, Mr. Ben, be so passionate and desperate. It was strange.

"Will you join my crusade? Will you help me catch the bad guys?"

Jill only had to think for a minute before she made up her mind. It didn't take a lot to convince her. She was on board the moment she heard Ben's story. The situation was the most dangerous one she'd ever be in. She might not be of any help. She might end up getting hurt or getting the professor hurt. Even after all that, she knew exactly what she needed to do. She knew she had to help the doctor. It was the absolute right thing to do.

"Yes."

Chapter 6: At the Bottom

The light from the laptop's screen was the only thing that lit up the dark room. Two people were sitting at the desk, concentrating on what was in front of them. Jill was typing on the computer, while Ben was shuffling through papers, strategizing. The Chinese takeout boxes, empty glasses of wine, and empty candy wrappers cluttered the desk along with Ben's documents.

Ben and Jill had spent many nights like these together. She had a habit of coming over to his place with a bottle of wine and some takeout in her hands. He wouldn't call it a ritual or tradition, because that meant there was some expected schedule for it, whereas Jill liked to surprise him most of the time. It had all started after Jill's probation period ended. She had received some bad news regarding her family and missed out on her interview with Ben. Ben liked to conduct such interviews with all his employees after their probation period just to understand them better and know how their experience had been thus far.

Jill had been so distraught that day that she had missed the day of work. For her, that was a big deal because she rarely ever took a day off. Ben had been surprised to learn that Jill had missed the day of work, and he called her to make sure everything was alright. After Jill explained to him about her family issues, Ben had understood and only been sympathetic to her plight.

That entire day of work felt even more burdensome to Ben because he wasn't used to Jill's absence at work. She was always there, keeping everyone positive and cheery. Her personality was addicting, and Ben was not afraid to say that he missed his friend. He didn't even realize how bad his mood was until Jacob talked to him.

"Um, boss," Jacob said hesitantly from the doorway of Ben's office. He looked nervous about stepping inside, and that confused Ben.

Since when did Jacob hesitate about anything?

"Yeah?" Ben asked.

"Can I talk to you?" Jacob asked and then rushed out, "If you're not busy, of course!"

"Of course, Jacob," Ben responded, confused by his behavior.

Jacob came inside and closed the door behind him. He got closer to the desk and looked unsure of how to start.

"Is everything okay, Jake?" Ben was concerned now.

"Yeah! I mean ... I don't know," Jacob muttered.

Ben frowned and raised an eyebrow.

"It's just that," Jacob sighed and looked up. "I was just wondering if everything is okay with you. Is there something wrong? Did someone mess up or something?"

"What?" Ben couldn't have been more confused.

Jacob started talking to Ben about his hot and cold behavior and how everyone was concerned they had done something wrong to make him upset. Ben felt terrible. He hadn't realized he was being so crappy, and he felt horrible about treating his employees that way. After he told Jacob that everything was fine and nothing had gone wrong, he went to each and every one of his employees to apologize for his behavior. He reassured them all that nothing was actually wrong, and they definitely hadn't done something wrong to make him upset.

That night, Ben was home, hanging out with Silice, when the doorbell rang. He thought it might be Dylan, because who else would drop in unannounced so late? When he opened the door, he was surprised to see Jill standing there with a small smile on her face and bags in her hands.

"Hey, doc," she greeted him, and he let her in.

"Jill? What are you doing here? Is everything okay?" Ben asked her.

"Everything's fine. Why? Can I not drop by once in a while?" Jill said lightly as she went to find the kitchen. "I have brought Chinese!" she yelled from the kitchen.

Ben was puzzled by her behavior. "What is going on?"

Jill turned to look at him and looked sheepish, "Okay, I'll explain. I spoke to Jacob earlier, and he told me about your pissy mood at work today. I felt kinda responsible for that since I thought that might have been because I took an unannounced off today. So, I have come bearing food and wine to apologize!"

Ben just stared at her in confusion, "I'm not mad, Jill."

"You're not?" Jill was the one who looked confused now.

"No, of course, not," Ben said. "You explained everything to me, and I understood. Why would I be mad?"

Jill smiled wide, "I'm glad."

"By the way, how is everything? You doin' okay?" Ben asked her as he helped her take out all the food she had brought. "You didn't have to do all this, though."

"I'm fine now. And yes, I did," Jill replied.

After gorging themselves on orange chicken and dumplings, Ben and Jill started talking seriously over their second glass of wine. She confided in him about her tough family situation, and Ben sympathized. In turn, he shared with her how he had been aggravated at work because he missed her sunny disposition.

"Aw, you missed me!" Jill giggled as she drank her wine till the last drop.

Ben chuckled, "I guess, yeah. I just didn't realize I had gotten so used to your presence at work. You do help keep things positive and light. I can be..."

As Ben tried to search for a word to explain his grumpy mood, Jill jumped in, "Brooding?"

"I was going to say serious, but sure," Ben drank his wine down.

They poured more wine and talked for hours. That night, Ben and Jill became closer friends, and Ben felt grateful that he had found such a good friend like her. Since then, Jill would often come over with food and wine. They would pig out on his couch and watch action movies. That had been another thing they bonded over. Apparently, Jill loved action movies as much as Ben. He was happy to have found a kindred spirit since Dylan always trashed his taste of movies.

However, now they had switched out Danny Tejo movies for poaching research. It was much more serious, but it still felt nice to hang out with Jill. Ben knew he had made the right decision to include her in his mission. He felt comforted not only by the thought of how skilled she was at finding things but also because she really was a good friend who understood him and was willing to support him with something so sensitive.

"So, Peter is the head of all things, right?" Jill asked once more to make sure she had the correct info.

"Peter is the kingpin. We take him down; we take down everything. The whole system is run by him. In order to do so, we have to find incriminating evidence to put Peter away for a long time and successfully end his business," Ben explained.

"That I get. But, how do you plan on getting that evidence?" Jill inquired curiously.

"Well, that's where you come in. I looked everywhere for any records, any trails that could lead to his illegal business, but I couldn't find anything. The guy has nothing in his records, not even a parking ticket," Ben said, running his hand through his hair frustratingly. "It was hard to even look for him. It's like he doesn't exist. He has created a fake identity to run this business, and now there's no evidence regarding that either. I couldn't find it, at least."

Jill raised an eyebrow at that.

"Which is why you are here. I was hoping that with your expertise and skills, you could maybe find something about him. Anything that could paint him in the wrong light," Ben finished.

"Look, doc," Jill pushed her glasses up her head and perched them on top of her hair. "Finding info on Peter is not going to be hard, but if he is as squeaky clean as you say he is, then it might be difficult to gather enough evidence to build a case against him. What we find can be, at most, circumstantial. But we need more," Jill said.

"What do you want me to do then?" Ben asked.

"Going after Peter is like looking for a needle in a haystack. I say we hit pause on that," Jill suggested.

"Hit pause? Jill, I can't do that! I've worked on this for years! How can you ask me to hang my hat?" Ben exclaimed.

"Would you calm down? I didn't say you should stop. I'm saying don't go after something that will take time and energy that can be spent on something more fruitful. I have an idea," Jill said calmly.

Ben just waited for her to elaborate.

"What if we went after someone who was easier to catch? Someone who works for Peter but is not so squeaky clean. Once we catch him, we can get him to spill on Peter. That would be quicker and easier than looking for stuff against Peter ourselves," Jill elaborated.

"That ... actually sounds good. How do we go about it?" Ben was intrigued.

"It's simple really. We find the weakest link and break the chain. The weakest could be at the bottom. Someone who is not really that high up in ranks but is still a part of the business enough to know about Peter's dealings. Someone ... new perhaps," Jill mused.

As Jill typed on her laptop furiously, Ben just waited for her to continue. She was smart, and what she did right now just proved it. What she had said was brilliant, because it would help Ben gain information from an insider, not an outside source. This would make sure that he gets to Peter, slow and steady.

"Found it!" Jill brought Ben out of his thoughts. "There is some new guy named Rahul who has joined his team recently. It says here that he is a new business partner, but, of course, we know what that means."

"Wait? You have found out who we need to go after first? Already?" Ben was surprised.

"Yeah, only took a few clicks," Jill answered.

Ben was really grateful to have her on his side.

Hours later, after a few containers of Chinese food and half a bottle of wine, they had pinned down Rahul. Jill had learned that Rahul was masquerading as a veterinarian. That information had almost made Ben ballistic, but he reined it in.

"So, since he is a vet like you, do you know him?" Jill asked.

"Not all veterinarians know each other, Jill," Ben said exasperatedly.

"Just wondering," Jill typed at her keyboard more. "Oh! He does have a connection with you!"

Ben was shocked, "How?"

"He went to the same alma mater as you," Jill explained.

"That's surprising," Ben mused.

Ben started doing his own research on his laptop to find out more about this Rahul who had apparently gone to the same school as him. After a little bit of digging, Ben and Jill were able to find that Rahul was someone who went out in the jungle along with Peter sometimes. He would use his persona as a vet to locate wild animals.

"It's like a serial killer looking for his victims as a doctor," Jill shook her head. "But, Ben, if you go after him, it might be dangerous."

"We have to. We have no other choice. Without going after Rahul, we can't get to Peter. To do that, I have to follow him in the hunt," Ben decided.

"Yes, but this guy seems strong. If he fights you, then you're gone," Jill was staring at the picture of Rahul she had pulled up on her screen. The man was a brown-eyed, dark-haired block of muscle. There was no other way to describe it. He had tattoos on his hands, one on his bicep, and his entire aura screamed danger. His face belied a coldness that was hard to miss.

"Jesus, what made people think he's a trustworthy vet to take care of their pets?" Jill commented.

"He looks exactly like the kind of guy who would be okay with something as evil as poaching. And just as cold-blooded as Peter," Ben said.

"So, how will you go up against this guy? With your scalpel? Or your puppy scrubs?" Jill asked humorously.

"I have some experience in combat, you know," Ben said.

"Really? And what kind of combat is that?" Jill was still unsure.

"Karate. I took classes when I was younger. I'm a black belt," Ben said proudly.

Jill gasped, "Dude! That's so amazing! You're so badass!"

Ben thought back to his karate days.

***

"Again!" The instructor yelled at Ben.

Ben was exhausted and his limbs were screaming, but he kept going.

"Again!" His instructor was not going to let him slack.

Again and again, Ben kicked and learned the moves he needed to without complaints. He knew that it was all a part of his journey. A journey to catching some bad guys.

Ben had always been the brains instead of brawn. Even in school, he never enjoyed the physical activities as much as the biology club.

He was labeled a "nerd" by many, but he didn't mind it. He was always the smart one. Even if he would get bullied, he would get out of it by outsmarting the others. He never thought he would be someone who would willingly want to learn karate, a hard combat technique.

Learning karate was not the hardest part. It was the discipline that came with it. Even though it was about combat, karate teaches you to be level-headed and calm at all times. You cannot lose your cool. That had never been difficult for Ben, but whenever he thought about Peter or the people who followed in his footsteps, Ben had a hard time keeping cool. Learning karate was his way of making sure that he covered all his bases and didn't leave a loophole for the enemy. He was going to take Peter down, even if he had to get his hands dirty.

***

Ben was prepared and ready to follow Rahul. Jill had gotten a ping of his location and learned that he was going hunting early morning. Ben immediately got ready, knowing this was his chance to catch him. He was dressed in camouflage. He had made sure to cover all his tracks, figuratively and literally. He couldn't let Rahul get away or get spooked into hiding, so Ben had to make sure that his disguise was perfect.

"Woah, look at you, doc!" Jill said appreciatively. "Or actually, not look at you, because you've done it so well! I can't even tell you're there."

Ben chuckled at Jill's ridiculousness.

"You're just full of surprises, huh?" Jill smirked. "First, karate. Now, this. What other things are you hiding up your sleeve, doc?"

"Can we go now?" Ben said, not wanting to waste time.

Jill nodded and they were off. They had taken the van from the clinic to remain inconspicuous. Jill decided to set up a shop in the back of the van so that she could be Ben's eyes and ears while he was out, catching Rahul. She set up her surveillance and other equipment, making Ben appreciate having her on his team once more. He would've never been able to do this. As they parked near the spot where Rahul was supposed to be, Ben and Jill lay in wait for him to make some move. Once they spotted Rahul trekking his way through the forest, Ben got ready to go after him.

"Just be careful, doc. I know you know karate and whatnot, but this is still a criminal — a dangerous one," Jill warned.

Ben nodded and left the van quietly. After following Rahul's footsteps quietly through the forest, Ben waited for him to take a break. He was careful not to step on any twigs or leaves so as not to alert Rahul of his presence. Rahul remained oblivious to Ben's presence alongside him. Finally, after an hour or so, Rahul took a break and sat down on a fallen tree to drink water and take deep breaths. "This is it, doc. This is your chance," Jill said in Ben's ear.

He was wearing a communications device in his ear so that Jill and Ben could remain in contact. It was to make sure Jill could save him if there were any problems. Ben took a deep breath and went to crouch behind a tree. He was waiting to see if Rahul would get up and move or remain sitting. When Rahul didn't move, Ben shook out his limbs, took another deep breath, and recounted all the *instructions his old instructor had taught him. He imagined his instructor sitting right next to himself at that moment and telling him what he needed to hear.*

"It's not about hurting him. It's about rendering him immobile and unable to come at you. You don't have to hurt him. You were trained for this, Ben. I have faith in you," the imaginary instructor said in his head.

"Ben? Just so you know, I totally believe in you. You're a badass, and you can take on Rahul any day," Jill said in his ear.

Ben chuckled after detecting a hint of nervousness in her voice, "It's okay, Jill. I'll be fine. Don't worry, this won't take too long."

Right as he said that, Ben made his move. He swiftly crept behind Rahul, remaining silent, and then suddenly hit him on the side of his head. Rahul groaned and clutched his head in pain as he reached for Ben with his other hand. "What the hell," Rahul's speech was garbled, the hit taking immediate effect. He wasn't going to go down easily though. Rahul stood up on shaky legs, turned around, and finally spotted his silent attacker. He reached out to punch Ben, who managed to dodge it. Then Rahul became desperate, reaching out with both hands and running up to Ben. Ben backed up on a tree, and Rahul grabbed him by his neck. He started choking Ben, as he gasped and struggled for breath.

"Ben?! Ben, are you okay?!" Jill screamed in his ear.

Ben was being choked by hundreds of pounds of muscles, but he wasn't panicking. He knew that the way he had hit Rahul, he would be unconscious in a minute or so. As Rahul kept choking Ben, Ben just counted the minutes in his head. Suddenly, Rahul's hands became loose around his throat, and, soon enough, Ben heard a thud as the man fell down. Ben coughed and struggled to catch his breath.

"I'm fine, Jill. He's out," Ben wheezed into the mike.

"Oh, thank god! I thought he killed you!" Jill exclaimed in relief.

"So much for your faith in me," Ben chuckled.

***

As Rahul blinked his eyes open, he felt his mind coming back to the land of the living. His eyes took a long time to open; his mouth felt like it was sewn shut; it was so dry, and there was a painful throbbing at the back of his head that made him wince as soon as he opened his eyes. After blinking and trying again, he finally opened his eyes to a strange sight.

"Who the hell are you?" Rahul croaked as he saw that he was faced with a pretty, blonde girl who was staring at him curiously. "You couldn't have been the one who knocked me out."

Rahul also noticed that he couldn't move his legs or arms. He was in a chair, with his arms tied behind his back and his legs tied to the chair's legs.

"What is this, some sort of sorority prank? Why the hell am I tied?" Rahul glowered at Jill. Jill remained unfazed, knowing he couldn't do anything. Suddenly, a different voice spoke out from behind Rahul.

"You're here because of the things you've done, Rahul," Ben said.

Rahul tried to turn around and look at who was talking, but he couldn't.

"Who the hell are you and why did you kidnap me?"

"We didn't kidnap you. We'll let you go once you answer a few questions for us," Ben finally came into Rahul's line of sight. "You work for Peter, right?"

Rahul was confused, but he was slowly catching on, "Who are you?"

"I'm the one asking the questions. So, Peter?" Ben said.

Rahul laughed. "You think I'll answer you? Why?"

Ben suddenly came close enough to whisper in Rahul's ear as he grabbed the hair on the back of his head, right where his wound was, making Rahul wince and hiss in pain. "You'll answer me because I'm the one who's calling the shots. I can snap your neck with one slight twist of my hand. I know how to break bones."

Rahul remained quiet, knowing he couldn't go anywhere. "What the hell do you want from me?"

"You work for Peter, right?" Ben asked again, stepping back to stare down at him.

"Yes," Rahul said.

"What do you do for him?" Ben asked.

"I'm his go-to man for every animal he needs. I scout them, and he hunts them," Rahul said.

"Wow, he's an easy one to crack," Jill commented from behind.

Ben turned back to Rahul and asked, "I want to take him down. What do you have on him?"

Rahul laughed again, "You think I'll just hand over evidence about Peter?"

"If you value your life, yes," Ben was bluffing. He could never hurt someone, but Rahul didn't need to know that.

"If you want to get to Peter, you have to find him first. Catch him in the act, perhaps," Rahul suggested.

"How do we do that?" Ben asked.

"You get close to him. And the only place you can find him is the jungle," Rahul said.

Ben and Jill just stared at each other. Then Ben turned around to Rahul and said one last thing.

"You'll tell me exactly where to find him. Where he'll go next. Or else, you know what I'm capable of."

Rahul just stared at Ben and saw the knife he was holding that he hadn't noticed the first time. He gulped and then nodded.

"Okay.

Chapter 7: In the Jungles

When Dana was young, around nine years old, she met a friend named Steve. Steve's family had just moved in next door to the Harpers, and Dana was excited to see that they had a child her age. Both the families encouraged the two to become friends since they had started getting along so well.

One day, Steve's mother came to the Harper house, holding hands with her nine-year-old son, Steve. Mrs. Harper opened the door to be met with a strange and unfamiliar face.

"Hello? May I help you?" Dana's mother, Candice, asked.

"Hi! I am Shirley Robinson. We just moved in next door!" Shirley said with a wide, friendly smile that immediately put Candice at ease.

Shirley was a robust woman with shiny, black hair; crystal blue eyes; and a slightly tan complexion. Her son mirrored her features, with his shiny, black hair; blue eyes; and a tan.

"Oh, hello! I heard the Cavanaugh's moved out. It's nice to meet you, Shirley," Candice reached out to shake hands with Shirley. She asked Shirley to enter and took her to the living room. After serving Shirley some iced tea and her son a glass of cold apple juice, Candice sat down to start to get to know her new neighbors.

"And who is this young fellow?" Candice stared at the boy who shyly held on to his mother's skirt and only looked up when he thought no one was looking.

"This is my little Steve," Shirley said adoringly, patting her son's head. We just celebrated his ninth birthday in Georgia before we moved here."

"Oh, you're from Georgia? How's California treating you so far?" Candice started to make a conversation.

"It's been really good. We love the sun, obviously," Shirley chuckled.

As the women kept chatting, Steve looked around shyly. He was always a shy boy, hesitant to talk to other people. Suddenly, a young brunette came bouncing down the stairs, and Steve looked away shyly. As Dana paused at the sight of the guests, her mother introduced her to Shirley and her son.

"Oh, this is my daughter, Dana. She is also nine, like your Steve," Candice said with a smile.

Shirley started talking to Dana. She loved how the young girl was so outspoken, confident, and smart even at such a young age.

"This is my son, Steve. Steve, say 'hello,'" Shirley introduced the kids to each other.

"Hi, Steve! How are you?" Dana immediately started being friendly with the boy, who only looked down with red cheeks.

"Aw, he's a shy one, is he?" Candice said, endeared.

"Yeah, he's taken after his dad in that way," Shirley giggled. "Doesn't have many friends because of that."

Dana took it as a challenge. She wanted to bring Steve out of his shell and be friends with him. She couldn't imagine how he lived, having no friends in life to have fun with. She had a lot of friends. She was naturally good at socializing and making friends ever since she was a baby. She wanted to be friends with Steve too.

"Come on, Steve! I will show you my puzzle collection and trophies!" Dana said excitedly and then took him by the hand to drag him upstairs to her bedroom.

The mothers laughed at Dana's behavior, Shirley saying, "I would be so glad if they became friends, honestly. She could help him come out of his shell."

Candice nodded, "Yeah, my daughter loves making friends."

The next time Shirley and Candice met was when Candice baked a cherry pie for the new neighbors and took it to their house. Dana insisted on going along so she could meet Steve. After their first meeting, Steve had started to be vocal and less shy. Dana just had that effect on people. Steve was a very polite and soft-spoken boy once he did start talking. Though, he still kept mostly to himself and let Dana lead. Dana was intrigued by the boy. She couldn't understand what was going through his head at any time. She realized she wanted to know more about him.

As Candice and Shirley talked and ate pie together over a cup of coffee, Dana and Steve hung out in his room. Dana thought it was quite a boring room, for a boy at least. She expected to see a lot of sports or car memorabilia. She expected it to look like any other nine-year-old boy's room. But it was quite simple and didn't have much.

"I like it like this. Simple," Steve said quietly when Dana commented on how his room looked boring.

She shrugged, and they started to play board games. The more time she spent with Steve, the more interesting details started coming out. That day, she learned that Steve was quite the little champion of video games. He was so good that it looked like his fingers were blurring over the controller buttons. Dana was very surprised and impressed.

"You know, I am really good at puzzles. Do you like them?" Dana asked Steve after losing to him at video games fifth time in a row.

"Sure, but what do you like about them?" Steve asked her curiously.

"Well, I like the feeling I get when I solve them," Dana replied.

"That's it?" Steve asked.

"Yeah," Dana said. "The feeling that you have completed something and done it right feels very nice."

The kids had no idea how right they were in discussing the feeling of accomplishment. It was an intense feeling. A feeling that made people crave it and work for it to the extreme. After that day, Steve and Dana became really close friends. Their parents were happy, because they thought Dana was a good influence on Steve, and he seemed to be opening up more and more around her.

Dana liked being friends with Steve. Her friend, Jessica, once asked her why she was friends with someone like him who barely spoke or was so shy.

"He's nice. He can play video games very well too. Plus, he has been talking more and more around me. Every day, he gets more talkative and less shy. It's like … it's like he's a puzzle! And I am solving it," Dana smiled wide.

Jessica just rolled her eyes at that.

Dana's mother understood that her daughter felt like she was solving a puzzle when it came to Steve. He was so mysterious and shy that every day, Dana would try to get him to open up more, and when he did, it was like she had found another piece of the puzzle. She thought it was good for both of them because Steve could open up and be himself that way.

Years passed, and the friends grew up together. Everyone knew that Dana and Steve were best friends. They would go everywhere together and do everything together. They were inseparable. They were both in high school when Steve discovered something about himself.

"Dana, can I talk to you?" he said one evening.

"Sure," Dana responded.

Steve took her to the quietest corner he could find in the school hallways and started talking to her.

"I think I am adopted," Steve told her.

"What?" Dana was shocked. "Did your parents say that?"

"No, but I have a feeling," Steve replied.

"Wait, I don't get it. You look so much like your mother," Dana said, confused.

"I also look exactly like my aunt," Steve pointed out.

"So, that just proves you have their genes," Dana said. "Why do you even think that you're adopted?"

"It's just little things here and there. Stuff my parents say when they think I'm not listening. Or things that I have observed. I can't really explain it," Steve said.

"That's okay. I mean, if you feel like that, there must be some reason," Dana responded. "Do you think there's a way we can find out?"

"I have looked in my house for documents or things that could point toward it, but I haven't found anything," Steve told her with a sigh.

Dana noticed how her friend looked despondent. Even though it wasn't confirmed, she could understand how thinking he was adopted could make him feel sad or unwanted. She could tell Steve was sad, and because she couldn't stand seeing her friend sad, she said the next thing without thinking much about it.

"I'll do it," Dana said.

"Do what?" Steve was confused.

"I'll find out if you're adopted or not," she promised.

"How?" Steve asked.

"It will be like a puzzle. I will search for clues and pieces that could give us information. Then one by one, those pieces will start coming together, and we will solve the whole thing!" Dana said excitedly.

"You and your obsession with puzzles and mysteries!" Steve rolled his eyes and chuckled.

Dana started researching about Steve's parentage and worked hard on discovering the truth. Steve helped her with whatever she needed to find the answers. Nobody knew what they were up to, because they didn't want to raise any alarms without getting any confirmation.

It took her weeks, but Dana did eventually find out the truth regarding Steve's parentage. As it turned out, Steve had been right about how he felt. He was adopted. It broke Dana's heart to tell him the truth, but she knew he deserved to know that. Steve cried when she told him, but then he refused to wallow in misery. When Dana told him about who his parents really were, Steve was shocked.

"My aunt? Are you sure?" Steve asked Dana.

"Apparently, your aunt got pregnant by some boyfriend in high school. She didn't want an abortion or to give it up. Your parents were already married at the time and wanted to have a child. They told her that they would adopt the child so that she could remain a part of his life. It all turned out well for everyone," Dana told him.

After that, Steve went to talk to his parents about everything Dana had found out. They told him the same story and explained how they had immediately fallen in love with him as if he were their own. They never thought that he wasn't. Steve didn't have any hard feelings for his parents. He knew they loved him as much as a parent should. He never felt like they skimped on any love or made him feel unwanted. Though, he did want to talk to his aunt about everything.

When Steve broke the news to Dana that he was moving back to Georgia for a while to spend time with his birth mother, Dana was sad. She knew she couldn't stop him, but she didn't want to lose her best friend either. They made promises to keep in touch, but after graduating high school, they both got too busy with their lives, and their contact faded away.

When the time came for Dana to pick a career path and go to college to get a degree, she chose journalism. She knew journalism was all about solving puzzles and answering questions by digging deeper for information. It was something that called out to her, and she followed the calling. It reminded her of how she had helped Steve find out about his parentage, and she knew she had done a good job back then. She realized she was really good at it, so she wanted to try it out as a career.

Throughout her college and postgraduate days, she became quite a skilled journalist, always looking for answers to questions that others couldn't solve. She received much admiration and praise from her peers in academia for her brilliant skills. She figured that once she went on to establish her career, it would be even better, and she would get to do what she loved most. It was to no one's surprise that Dana Harper became one of the best journalists of her graduating class. A few years later, she got a position as a news reporter with the city's biggest new outlet, City Report. Working for such a big corporation, Dana felt like she was on the right path. She was doing what she loved most, and her job was actually fulfilling. She was doing things that were rewarding and important. That was why it didn't make much sense to her when she found herself being denied to do exactly that.

"Stephen! What is this? You swiped my piece for that Hollywood gossip trash?" Dana was furious as she marched into her editor's office bright and early.

"Well, good morning to you too, Dana. How are you doing this morning?" Stephen said with an unperturbed look on his face.

"Don't give me that," Dana threw her file on Stephen's desk. "I told you this was important."

Stephen sighed as he took off his round black spectacles. His bald head, blue bow tie, and crisp, white shirt gave him a boyish look, even though he was much older than Dana.

"Look, Dana. I have told you multiple times that we can only run a story if it has enough traction. Your article didn't even generate much buzz on the website. The 'Hollywood gossip trash' did," Stephen used air quotes.

Dana brushed off the few strands of hair that had come loose from her ponytail and crouched down to Stephen's level, pressing her hands against his desk, "I don't care, Stephen. You promised me you would run this story."

"That's because I didn't know it was about this!" Stephen pointed at the file Dana had thrown at his desk. "Seriously, Dana. No one really cares about illegal poaching as much as they want to know the latest Kardashian scandal."

Dana curled her fists and leaned back up to her full height, "That's because of people like you. If you care to show the damn truth, people might actually learn about things that are more important!"

"Look, I'm sorry, but you know how this works. I cannot, in good conscience, run a story that would simply make us lose ratings," Stephen put his glasses back on. "However, since I know how much this means to you, I'll make you a wager."

Dana was intrigued. She raised her eyebrow and crossed her arms against her chest, "What?"

"If you can bring me something about this story that clicks, something that grabs attention ... like who's running the operation. Or whoever's in charge. Maybe an interview with the person... Then I could consider running it," Stephen said.

Dana just stared at him, not one to back down from a challenge. "Fine," she agreed.

"Great!" Stephen grinned, and then Dana took her file and left the office.

Dana had come across illegal poaching and was surprised to find such damning evidence. There was a lot of information, including the names of people in high ranks. She was shocked that nobody really spoke much about this topic. There was so much information if someone just bothered to look. She knew that it wasn't enough to get the attention of authorities, but there was enough to ask tough questions. There was also the added benefit of shining light on such a severe and dangerous crime. Dana had learned that it ran much like a mob cartel. These people had built empires based on such heinous crimes. They had established a network, an industry. When she had seen pictures and videos, she was horrified to her core. These people were hurting beautiful endangered species just for their selfish material gain. It disgusted her.

Dana was great at research and had managed to unearth a lot of details about the seedy business, using her secret resources. Her investigation had led to her finding of Black Castle. At first, she thought it was a place, somewhere all these bad men met up — something like a headquarters. However, upon digging deeper, she discovered that it was a mysterious person attached to the entire organization. After getting challenged by Stephen, she knew she had to do more research and find a way to reach the leader of the entire operation.

Going home that day, Dana couldn't wait to get started on work. She lived alone, with only her pet cat to keep her company. Her work was her life. She barely went out and socialized. She started investigating illegal poaching a couple of weeks prior and felt like she was too busy to entertain friends or guests. That night, she went deeper in her research to find the person who was in charge, the one behind everything. She knew that if she could solve this puzzle, this mystery, it could be one of the most prominent cases to come to light, and that would be a huge accomplishment for her. She looked everywhere, and it wasn't until a little later that Dana came across Peter. She found his name attached to everything. They were using building golf courses as a cover for their business. Peter's name was attached as the main investor, but there was next to no information about him on the internet. At first, she thought it must have been a made-up name, but the deeper she looked, the more she realized it was not. Peter was a real person, with basically no records or signs of existence. He had a clean slate, which was suspicious, because it looked as if he had wiped everything with bleach.

Dana continued to work late into the night, looking at her cat and knowing that she would do anything to make sure this crime was brought to light. She had always been an animal lover. Since she always loved staying indoors, she became the perfect little girl to have pets. She had grown up taking care of animals. Her mother used to work in a veterinarian hospital. It was quite apparent that Dana was an animal lover. It was one of the reasons why she was so adamant about putting this story in the limelight.

The next few days were expended diligently researching and trying to uncover Peter's tracks. It wasn't much later that Dana discovered Peter had a loyal gang of minions. She knew from experience that if you were trying to take down an organization, a criminal one, you couldn't just go directly for the leader. You had to be strategic about it. If you went after the leader, they would use all their resources, including money, minions, and even dangerous methods, to keep you off their trails. Dana knew that she had to work her way up. She had to take away those resources before she went for the head because she knew that once she did that, Peter wouldn't be able to defend himself, let alone come after her. The first link she would dismantle would be his loyal minions. She would start by letting the weakest link in the chain break so that she could get a way. As she looked around, trying to find out who was the weakest link in Peter's network, she discovered that a new poacher had just joined his team.

A man named Rahul had just joined the roster of bad guys and started working with Peter. It didn't take her long to discover that he was kind of like a scout for Peter. Rahul would go out and scout the animals, come back to Peter with information, and then they would hunt together. She knew he was the weakest link because he was new. It meant that he didn't have any time yet to become loyal or important enough to Peter.

Dana had to get Rahul to spill on Peter, and she would be in. She tracked him down and realized that he was using a veterinarian persona to hide his true evil intentions. It was quite smart, even if a little disturbing. That was how Dana found herself scouting the city for vets who could possibly have a connection with Rahul. She figured maybe there was someone who knew him or worked with him — anyone who could point her in his direction. So, she was led to a young vet, Dr. Benjamin Morrison. He was quite popular due to his good work and how he was an avid animal rights activist. She didn't know why, but she had a gut feeling that she should meet him, because he was a connection, somehow. After their failed meeting, Dana was disappointed. She still didn't know why but she knew Ben was her link to Peter. She always trusted her gut feeling, so she was not arguing against it. Then she set out to find Rahul herself. Maybe she could catch him in the act. She started trailing him and found out that he was supposed to go scouting for Peter soon. Dana got ready to follow him and maybe take pictures and videos. She went out and headed to the jungle in hopes of finally catching a break in her story.

As she approached the jungle, she decided to try a new angle. She couldn't just follow Rahul because he was a trained hunter. He could catch on to her, and that could turn out badly for her. He seemed like the kind of guy who wouldn't mind hurting a woman if she was getting in his way. Dana was not scared. She knew danger was a constant part of her work. However, she was also not reckless. She knew she could try something different to catch Rahul and Peter by extension.

Dana discovered the tigers that Rahul was coming to scout, taking a second to marvel at their beauty. She felt her motivation renewed after seeing the beautiful, exotic animals in danger from such bad men as Rahul and Peter. She started circling the tigers from a safe distance, of course. She was smart. She knew that this was the proverbial gold chest, and anyone who wanted a piece would eventually come close. She was lying and waiting anxiously, anticipating a poacher to come by and do their thing to catch them in the act that would eventually lead to Peter. Much to Dana's disappointment, though, she waited for hours for any sign of illegal poachers, but none of them made an appearance. Even Rahul didn't follow up, which she found strange. She had seen him entering the jungle; why hadn't he reached the tigers yet? She shook it off and made her way out of the jungle before it got too dark.

Tired, hungry, and frustrated at the lack of anything she had gotten, Dana headed home. Upon reaching, she took a long hot shower and got a full meal inside her belly. Next, she sat down with her research. She was tired, yes, but she couldn't sleep until she solved the puzzle of how Rahul never made it to the tigers when that was what he intended to do that day.

Did he suddenly change his mind? Why? And if so, wouldn't Peter be enraged? Where did Rahul even go, because she hadn't seen him leave?

The night was spent trying to answer the questions that Dana had in her head. Her exhausted brain soon gave in to the sweet temptation of sleep, and she fell asleep on the couch, surrounded by her research files. It might seem sad, but that was her life. She could never leave a puzzle unsolved. She spent the next following days in her research, with Stephen coming by her office once to remind her of what he promised. She assured him that she would get him that break in the story that he wanted. She might have assured him, but she had no idea how to do it. Dana had tried to find Rahul's next mission and what he intended to do, but she could never trail him. It was like he had disappeared into thin air. She was very puzzled by that occurrence. Where did Rahul go that day? He didn't turn up again after that, and her carefully crafted lead had gone cold.

She spent hours trying to figure out where Rahul was. Maybe he was working secretly from a hidden, underground base. All she had were theories, and she couldn't pin down any one of them as to what might have really happened. After the trail had gone cold, she was left with no other option but to return to her original line of research — Peter.

Every moment when she was free, Dana was researching about Peter. She had to find him, and she wouldn't rest until she did. She exhausted her resources in trying to locate the man. One night, Dana got up to get her fifth cup of coffee from her kitchen, observing her cat Skittles, who was curled on the couch fast asleep. She had been working all night, and it was around three in the morning. She knew she was getting nowhere, but she had to keep looking. She couldn't give up.

As the warm coffee slid down her throat and gave her that bit of kick to open her eyes and focus on her work in front of her, Dana paused. Rahul was supposed to go scouting for Peter. She had trailed him that day, and he had disappeared. That meant the task was left unfinished. If Rahul was out of commission, since she couldn't find him after looking for him everywhere in the past week or so, Peter must still be looking for someone to scout for him. He couldn't let his business lag because of one poacher. He must have others on his team to help him out with that. That meant Dana was looking in the wrong place.

"Oh my god! Of course!" Dana exclaimed, startling Skittles, who glared at her, stretched, and walked off in the direction of her bedroom.

Dana had just come to a realization that the task was still left unfinished, so Peter must have delegated it to some other poacher by then. All she had to do was return to the site where Rahul had gone and wait for the next poacher to come by to finish Peter's work for him. It was quite obvious now that she thought about it. She felt excited because she finally had a lead after Rahul's trail had gone cold.

Knowing she couldn't waste any more time than she already had, Dana packed up her equipment, including a fancy, high-resolution camera, listening devices, and other things that she would need to stay hidden and safe in the jungle while scouting the poachers. She packed up her car and left for the jungle where she last had been.

Thankfully, Dana noticed that there didn't seem to be any signs of an illegal poacher dropping by in the last few days. She set up a camp, hidden behind bushes, and set up the angle to shoot the tigers from her camera. She would get everything on film.

As Dana sat, waiting for hours, she munched on the snacks she had brought with her. The last time she had been there, she had grown tired of waiting around, but this time, she was motivated because she knew someone would come by eventually. Sometimes, being a journalist meant just waiting to catch people in the act. It meant trailing and scouting for hours and even days. She had once followed a senator known to have been embezzling from the government's funds and spent three days waiting for him to come to the safe house where he stashed the money. It was all worth it, because when the story broke, everyone was surprised, and Dana grew higher up in the ranks.

It wasn't just the popularity or success that Dana was after in this very poaching case. This one was more important and meaningful because she was doing it out of a sense of responsibility and care for animals. She didn't care if she gained notoriety for it. She just wanted to bring justice to those people who thought harming animals for their selfish gains was a good business model.

Waiting in the jungle, Dana suddenly noticed a group of men in the distance. She grew alert and zoomed in with her camera to see who it was. It wasn't Peter or even Rahul — just a bunch of strange men who were disguised in camouflage. Dana felt her eyes widen. They were holding rifles and other equipment that looked like it could be used for poaching. Dana got ready to film them in the act. She sat waiting for them to make a move when they disappeared from her sight altogether. She looked this way and that but couldn't find them anywhere.

Dana figured they must have been men sent by Peter to finish Rahul's assignment. She was right. As she continued to try to look for them, she suddenly got an odd feeling that somebody was behind her. She paused and slowly turned around, only to be met with the barrel of a gun pointed in her face.

"Who the hell are you, lady?" a gruff voice asked.

It was one of the men she was looking for. They had found her, and now, she was in trouble. She didn't let them see that she was scared. She stood up, dusted off her pants, and spoke in a confident voice. "I am Dana Harper, and I know you work for Peter. I know what you came out here to do."

The men looked at each other quizzically and then back at her.

"You know Peter? And you think we work for him?" one of them asked.

Dana became confused at his confusion. "Well, of course. Why else would you be here?"

The men continued to look at each other in confusion until one of them stepped up, possibly the leader, and slowly lowered the gun aimed at Dana.

"I think there has been a misunderstanding," the man said with a polite smile. "You're Dana Harper? What are you, some private investigator or cop?"

"I am a reporter, actually," Dana said, still refusing to let them see she was a bit scared.

"Well, Dana Harper, it's so nice to meet you. I am Stan, and these are my men," the man said amicably. "We don't work for Peter. We are here to catch Peter."

Dana felt her eyes widen in shock, "What?"

"We came to catch him in the act because we have been looking for him for years. We knew if there was any place we could find him, it would be the jungle," Stan said.

To say that Dana was shocked would be an understatement.

"I think we're both after the same thing; catching Peter," Stan confirmed.

Dana and Stan sat down to discuss strategies after that, as his group continued to be on the lookout for Peter. They were animal rights activists and trying to bring justice and put Peter behind bars. As they talked, Dana was relieved to find herself in the company of these men. She was also thankful that they hadn't turned out to be Peter's men.

Later in the week, Dana received a call from Stan. He informed her that they had found Peter's base of operations. Dana was shocked because that was impossible information to gather, but these men were good. Even Dana had a hard time looking for that kind of information.

"We think you should join us this time, Dana," Stan said on the phone.

Dana was definitely intrigued and wondered if this was her opportunity to finally find Peter and bring him to justice. She knew Stan and his men were her best options to finally infiltrate Peter's network and expose his dirty deeds.

Chapter 8: Rescue

The darkroom was full of computer screens of all sizes. The walls, the tables, even part of the floor were covered in computers. Some of the screens displayed the CCTV footage from around the perimeter, while some displayed other things. People with headphones on were focused and working on their computers, chatting among themselves regarding what they were working on.

Soon, the door of the room opened, and it was none other than Peter — the man who so many people were after. He was wearing a crisp, blue suit with a red tie and a white shirt, looking more like the CEO of a Fortune 500 company rather than the leader of a poaching ring.

"Boys!" Peter greeted everyone in the room loudly. When a few of the girls raised their heads and looked at him disapprovingly, he quickly modified his greeting. "And girls; of course, can't forget the girls. I'm sorry, ladies," Peter gave them all a charming smile that they ignored.

"Why the hell is it so dark in here?" Peter said to no one in particular and went to open the blinds on the windows. As soon as he did that, the room was lit up with sunlight streaming in through the huge windows.

The computer techs all groaned and squinted after not being used to the light for so many hours. They complained and whined in annoyance, some even muttering curses.

"Oh, come on! You guys are gonna turn into vampires any day now. We need some light in this room," Peter said to everyone. "Especially since I come bearing news."

Everyone stopped working immediately and turned toward Peter with attention.

"We have something big coming up. Something bigger than anything we've ever done," Peter grinned wide. "I need you all to be on your best behavior and top-notch skills for this one."

As Peter continued to brief his group of tech geniuses inside his base of operations, there was a group of people just outside. These people weren't among the ones who worked for Peter. These people were the ones who had come for Peter.

The group was that of the same men who had come across Dana and asked her to join their team. They found Dana and knew she could be an asset to their team because of her vast knowledge and resources. She was also a strong and ferocious woman who could hold her own. She would be a great help to catch Peter.

Dana had agreed to the group's offer but on her own conditions. She had told them about Ben, and, after doing some research, she had found him to be an intriguing character. For some reason, she felt Ben would help her get to Peter. She still had no idea about Ben's mission to apprehend Peter. The group had agreed to Dana's terms, willing to give her and this Ben guy the benefit of the doubt. They told Dana about their plan of action and how they were going to invade Peter's base of operations.

Their plan was foolproof, and Dana knew it would work because the guys were good at what they did. However, she still wanted to meet Ben first and try to talk to him. As the group decided that they had to go and scout Peter's base, Dana told them she would go talk to Ben. They went their separate ways as the guys made their way to Peter's hidden base. It was deep into the woods, which made sense since Peter could go and do his dirty business and come back without anyone getting to know his ways.

Stan and his loyal teammates arrived at Peter's location easily enough. They were good at keeping under the radar and making sure no one could follow them. They were scattered around the perimeter to see how the security detail worked. They were going to watch and observe because they had to take notes for when they came back a few days after to invade Peter's space. They sat around for hours, waiting and watching in silence while communicating with each other over radio devices quietly. As they saw, many guards were stationed around the entire property.

Stan knew that his men would not be able to get in without being noticed. The security was so tight around the entire property that it made it nearly impossible for it to be invaded by any external forces. However, Stan was a professional. He knew that he could breach this property. It would just take a few extra resources, weapons, and a lot of strategy, but he could do it. As they watched, they saw a huge truck come in through the driveway. It stopped at the gate to be verified, and then the guards let it in.

The truck was huge. It was obvious that it was carrying some large shipment inside the container on the truck. The whole container was covered with a large tarp, concealing it from the view of others.

"Guys, do you see that? Does anyone have any eyes on what's inside?" Stan said through the radio.

A chorus of "No, boss" followed, letting him know that it was impossible to see what was in the truck.

To his intrigue, Stan also noticed that the truck was moving slowly. As if what it was carrying was heavy in weight.

"Weapons?" A man radioed to Stan.

"Could be," Stan knew that a man like Peter must have been armed to his teeth for running an operation as illegal as this one. He also knew to tread carefully.

"Should I try to take a look?" Stan's man said as the truck stopped in the driveway. It had been left behind as the driver and other men went inside.

"There are too many guards," Stan observed. It was highly telling that whatever was in the truck was of a lot of importance since there were around five men stationed around the truck, guarding it and keeping a sharp eye on their surroundings. "I don't know, guys. We only came here to observe."

"We should at least gather intel," one of his men said.

"It's too risky...," Stan knew the risks, but he would agree that leaving without gathering such important intel would also be stupid.

"We're here already..." said one of his men.

As two of Stan's men stepped toward the truck while remaining silent as the night and creeping in the shadows; Stan held his breath. Suddenly, a sharp sound as a twig broke in the bushes and alerted a guard near the truck. He immediately alerted his partner, and they both were on high alert. They held their guns, and one of them approached the bush to check what it was. Suddenly, Stan's man jumped out and knocked him out cold by hitting him on the head with the butt of his gun.

Stan and his group of men all jumped out at once and attacked the surprised guards who were standing around the truck. Since the driveway was a bit hidden from the view of the rest of the compound, the other guards around the perimeter couldn't see Stan and his men attacking. They silently took out the guards, fighting each one and trying to subdue them without having to kill. However, some had to be shot since both the opponents had a gun, and neither was budging.

Stan saw a guard, bleeding from his head, trying to rush inside and radio someone when he quickly fired and shot him squarely in the head. They all used their pistols with the silencers on them so they wouldn't alert the other guards around the property. However, they were too late, and before they could peek inside the truck and underneath the tarp, floodlights came on all around the property as a loudspeaker suddenly blared, "Intruder alert! Intruder alert!"

As Stan and his men rushed out of there, trying to stay hidden so they wouldn't get shot at by the guards rushing around everywhere, he realized he did need help with strategizing their invasion.

***

Dana met Ben that night, and to his surprise, she was straightforward in asking about Peter. She didn't want to beat around the bush, and Ben was surprised.

Ben asked, "How do you know about his illegal activities?"

Dana gave him a lengthy and detailed explanation of how she had found out about him when she was doing her piece on illegal poaching. After Ben learned of the whole story, he was more than a little impressed by Dana's drive to catch Peter.

Then Ben started telling Dana the story of how he got involved in the industry of illegal poaching at such a young age. He told her everything and about how he had been working on catching Peter for so many years. How his life and career had one primary goal — to catch Peter.

Dana was shocked, to say the least. She could understand why such a heart-wrenching tale had made Ben the way he had become—so driven to catch Peter and end his business.

"So, we catch him, using Stan and his group, and then we build a case against him using my resources, and bam! The witch is dead," Dana said with a smirk as they sat around planning.

"I don't know about the arresting part...," Ben said hesitantly.

"What? You don't want him to get arrested?" Dana asked, confused.

"I just don't think it'll be enough," Ben said.

"What do you mean?" Dana inquired, not sure what Ben was trying to say.

"Well, after the things he's done, he should definitely be apprehended by the law, of course. But do you really think Peter would get the punishment he deserves? With his connections and resources, I'm sure he'll get away with a minor sentence. Then what would be the point of all this?" Ben explained.

"Yes, but the most we can do is try to get him to put away for a long time. We'll get the best lawyers," Dana tried to assure him.

"No! You don't get it!" Ben exploded. "Even if we tried the hardest, Peter will get away. Either with a short sentence, probation, bail, or whatever his team of best-bought lawyers can conjure up."

Dana stared at him for a beat or two, then asked, "So, what do you suggest we do? Let him get away with it?"

"Of course not! I think we should think about what the best punishment for him would be at this point," Ben stated.

"And what is that?" Dana asked suspiciously.

"Maybe we should just ... kill him," Ben mumbled.

Jill had been watching their exchange silently, not wanting to interrupt, but at this point, she jumped out of her chair, "What?! You want to kill him?"

"Why not? He's committed murder, too. He should get the same punishment," Ben argued.

"That's not up to us to decide!" Dana finally said. "We cannot just kill him! That's not doing the right thing!"

"The right thing is for him to be put away for life! But that's not going to happen, now is it?" Ben seemed upset.

"Look, Ben," Dana sighed. "I get that this is personal for you. I do, believe me. But if we kill Peter, how does that make us any different than him?"

Ben stared at the wall as Jill looked at him with pleading eyes. Dana stepped closer to Ben and put a hand on his arm.

"Ben, please look at me."

When Ben finally turned her way, she gave him a soft, reassuring smile that spoke volumes and seemed to calm him down.

"We are going to get him. I promise. We will not fail," Dana assured Ben. "And if you are worried about him getting away scot-free, well, then don't be. I will personally make sure that man's life is ruined."

As Ben and Dana stared at each other for a few seconds, Jill cleared her throat to interrupt their moment, "Um, I am with Dana. We save lives, doc, not end them. We're not here to be killers."

After the girls had calmed Ben down, they started talking more, and soon enough, they diverted from the topic of Peter. They started discussing personal lives and stories, getting to know and learning more about each other. Ben and Jill knew each other fairly well, but Dana was a new addition to their team. They both seemed more than impressed to learn of how Dana seemed so driven and goal-oriented. They understood why she became a journalist.

"Man, I'm so glad you came to see doc. We needed another lady around here," Jill joked.

"What, am I getting too boring for you, Jill?" Ben asked, amused.

As the three caught up and learned more about each other, the night passed fairly soon. Jill and Dana seemed to bond over their shared level of skills when it came to finding answers. They both liked to look for things and solve mysteries. They both had the drive to find answers to questions, no matter how deep they had to go to find them.

"Have you ever been on the dark web?" Jill asked Dana.

"Once," Dana said and then shuddered as she thought about it. "It wasn't the best experience, but I had to look for a criminal who was hiding out on a platform there."

"Did you find him?" Jill asked curiously.

"Of course, I did," Dana said confidently.

"I am a frequent visitor of the dark web," Jill said, and Dana stared at her uncomfortably. "No! I mean, to look for things.

Like you! I sometimes go there to find some of the criminals and then silently report them to the authorities."

"Like an internet vigilante?" Ben chuckled.

"Something like that," Jill smirked. "But it helps me feel better. The things I see on there... Those people deserve much worse sometimes."

"That's true. I remember there was a woman who was arrested in Florida, and she was this really old lady. She lived a quiet life and had done nothing worse in her life than a parking ticket. Everyone was confused when she got arrested. The community felt she was being framed for some crime, so they petitioned to get her released on bail. Nobody actually knew what she was being arrested for," Dana told them.

"What was she arrested for?" Jill asked.

"Running a prostitution ring and cooking meth in her greenhouse," Dana replied.

"Oh, my God," Ben and Jill were both surprised.

"Yeah, she was caught through the dark web, because that's usually where she ran her business and got clients. Once the community learned of it all, they were horrified. They used to trust their children in her care, letting her babysit for hours. Safe to say, her sentence was increased after they all petitioned for it," Dana finished telling her story.

"That's just horrible. People are horrible," Jill made a face.

A little while later, Dana received a call from Stan. He told her about what happened at Peter's compound, and she was shocked. She relayed the information to Ben and Jill and put Stan on speaker so he could talk to everyone. Stan relayed the information to the rest of them, and Ben was more than shocked.

"Did you get to see what it was?" Ben asked hurriedly.

"No, we couldn't. Even though we fought with many of them and even killed some of them, but no. We were surrounded," Stan said.

There was a heavy silence blanketing the room. Jill, Ben, and Dana all looked at each other, wondering what to say to such news.

"How ... many did you kill?" Ben asked hesitantly.

"I don't think you wanna know, doctor," Stan said with a sigh.

Before the heaviness could settle more, Dana decided to change the subject, "So, now that you're done with recon, when should we invade?"

Stan replied, "A week later. I don't want them on high alert, which they will be after tonight."

As they talked more with Stan, they all came together to plan the invasion of Peter's base. With Jill's tech skills, Ben's drive and passion, Dana's intelligence, and Stan's militant skills, they came up with a plan that seemed perfect. They talked more afterward to hash out the details, and in the next two weeks, the team was busy preparing for the invasion.

"You're sure this would work, right? We've never done this before, doc," Jill said as she helped Ben put on his camo makeup. He was covered head to toe in camouflage clothing, hat, and gear. It was just his face that was visible, which he covered up with face paint. The greens, browns, and beiges of his entire ensemble made for the perfect camouflage outfit so that he could go in and out without being seen.

"Of course, it will, Jill. Don't worry. We'll catch him tonight," Ben assured him.

According to their plan, Ben was supposed to go first. They had fought over that detail a lot, but due to his insistence, he won out against everyone else. Nobody wanted to put the doctor in danger, but he was adamant that he could get in without any trouble. Jill confirmed, albeit begrudgingly, that Ben was good at hand-to-hand combat and could hold his own very well. Stan decided to help him finesse those skills. They had spent the last week training to get Ben even more in shape than he already was.

As the team arrived at the location, everyone got out and spread out to their locations, with Jill staying in the van, because that's where all her equipment and gadgets were. She would be monitoring them from inside the van, being their eyes and ears since they were going in the dark, literally! Then Stan and his men spread out around the perimeter, making sure they were in the right spots to eliminate any oncoming danger to the doctor as he went in. Ben was the one who would make a move and go inside using his camouflage and crawl through the darkened compound. He would enter through the hidden door of the basement and find his way in. Dana was supposed to stand back and see that Ben got inside without raising any alarms.

As the team did what it was supposed to, they all felt relieved that no guard was alerted as Ben made his way across the compound toward the basement. He managed to successfully crawl inside the door, after which Dana gave the signal that said he was in. Dana, Stan, and his team would follow behind just as silently while two men stood back to guard and make sure they could come out safely too.

After Jill managed to find the blueprints of the base, they were able to know that Peter's business took place underground. The basement through which Ben had crawled was where he had kept the animals in cages and cells. The plan was, Dana would go after him and take pictures and videos, as evidence of all the animals Peter kept locked away illegally. Then they would make their way through the underground hallways to the tech room where Peter usually was. However, as Ben walked through the basement, he saw something that made his hair stand on end. Dana followed behind him and stumbled into his back as he stood frozen in the middle of the huge basement/prison for animals.

"What's going on, Ben? Why did you stop?" Dana asked, confused.

What had made Ben freeze was the absolute absence of any animals in the basement.

"This is impossible! He always keeps them here!" Dana said, shocked.

"What? What's happening? It's too dark; I can't see!" Jill complained through the device in their ears.

"There are no animals, Jill," Dana mumbled. "We were wrong. He must have transferred them somewhere else. How are we supposed to gather evidence now? We can't just take Peter. That won't do anything!"

Dana's frustration was representative of what everyone felt at that moment. Then Stan's men, who were on guard outside, alerted them that someone was coming.

"We need to move out. Fast," Stan spoke in a hurry.

The group rushed out of the basement, feeling frustrated and hopeless at the twist in this tale. As they ran out, they happened to get separated in the hallway that was more like a maze. Stan and Dana went left, while Ben ran to the right.

As Ben ran, out of breath from running in the hallways that seemed to never end, he turned to see if the others were catching up, only to realize that none of them was there. Then he heard oncoming footsteps, so he decided to hide in the first room he saw. Getting inside the room, Ben blinked his eyes at the sudden attack of bright, white lights and turned to see where he had come. The room was huge. It looked like a garage but had the capacity of around ten cars. However, there was only one vehicle present at that moment. It was the same truck that Stan had seen coming to the compound a week ago. The tarp was still covering the truck, and that raised Ben's curiosity. He stepped toward the truck and, in a sweeping motion, took off the large sheet of tarp covering it. What he saw made him gasp out loud.

"Ah, so I see you've discovered it—my treasure, my golden hen," a voice said from behind him, and Ben turned to look, his eyes still wide from shock.

"How could you?!" Ben screamed out at Peter, who stood right in front of him, smirking like the cat who ate the mouse.

"How could I what?" Peter asked innocently while checking out his nails.

Ben pointed to the beautiful large tiger that was chained inside the cage covered with the tarp. The tiger was unconscious, and it looked so lonely and innocent in the big cage that was meant to imprison him forever, or for however long Peter needed him.

"Oh! Right," Peter said as if just realizing that he had a tiger locked up inside a cage. "Yeah, I couldn't resist."

At Peter's shrug, Ben charged at him full force, punching him repeatedly and taking out all the pain, frustrations, and hopelessness that he had caused all these years. As Ben continued to beat him up, Peter didn't defend himself and just laughed.

"Look at you," Peter said between gasping breaths. "You're so stupid. Here you have the chance to rescue that tiger and run, and yet, you are wasting it on me."

Ben paused as his vision cleared from the red haze of rage he flew in when he saw Peter. He was right. It was just him and Peter there, no other guard or armed man who could stop Ben. So, why was he wasting this time?

Ben looked back at the truck, the innocent, helpless tiger chained inside the cage, and then back at Peter, who was smirking like the evil man he was. Ben spit on his face to wipe that smirk off and then got up. He rushed to the truck, starting it in time and getting ready to flee with the endangered animal. He looked back at Peter once more, knowing he had the chance to kill him right then and there, but he had made a vow—a vow to protect all life, and especially the innocent animals who were in danger. This was not the time to be reckless. With his fists clenched around the steering wheel, Ben peeled out of the garage as the sound of Peter's deranged cackles followed him. No matter what, he stayed true to himself. Ben had saved a life instead of taking one, and he was more than okay with that.

Chapter 9: Hunted

As the tires squealed out of the driveway, Peter stood back, smirking. A group of his henchmen came running inside the garage, shocked at the sight of Ben driving away with their precious cargo in the truck. Peter turned to them directly and said, "Well, what are you waiting for? Go! Catch him!"

For a moment, everyone stood by, not understanding what was happening.

"I let him get a head start and figured it was the polite thing to do," Peter said, the smirk not leaving his face. As no one moved to follow the orders, he sighed. "Am I speaking Latin? Go!"

Immediately, the men started rushing toward the jeeps and vans parked inside the garage to run after Ben and catch him. Peter stood by—laughing, amused by the fact that Ben thought it would be so easy. Meanwhile, as Ben drove out of the garage, he radioed the team and told them to meet him at the back entrance. As he reached the big metallic gates of the property's backside, he saw the team was waiting for him there. They all climbed into the truck, panting and gasping after running and fighting off Peter's men.

"How did you get away?" Stan asked while he tried to catch his breath.

Ben stayed quiet for a moment, then told everyone what had transpired back at the garage between Peter and him.

"You saw him? Why didn't you shoot him?!" Stan asked, perplexed at how Ben could just let the guy go.

"It was either him or the tiger!" Ben exclaimed. "I do not regret choosing the tiger."

Then there was silence in the truck as Ben drove fast. Jill was following behind them in Ben's truck, keeping track of the group through GPS. As Ben drove through the empty road, he realized he had no idea where he was or where they were heading.

"Where is this road leading to?" Ben asked with confusion.

"I don't think this was on the map. I studied it; I should know," Stan was also confused.

"This must be how he's managed to escape all these years. These hidden roads," Dana figured.

"Guys, I don't think we're heading back to mainland...," Jill's voice said through the radio.

"Where are we going, Jill?" Ben asked her.

"I don't see this on the map. Not even Google Maps is showing this place," Jill's confusion was obvious through her voice.

"Dammit!" Stan exclaimed.

Ben kept driving, hoping they would somehow end up at the same road they had used to come to Peter's compound. However, it seemed more and more impossible as the road continued endlessly. They were anxious, hoping to get away as soon as possible. Suddenly, the flashing lights of another car behind the truck made Ben snap his attention to the rearview mirror. There was not one but many jeeps right behind the group.

"Peter's men," Stan observed.

Ben stepped harder on the gas, hoping to outrun them before they caught up to them.

"This is why you should've shot him," Dana said, watching the jeeps in the rearview mirror as they slowly closed the distance.

"I knew he wasn't going to just let me drive off with the tiger," Ben said wryly.

As he kept increasing the speed, he noticed a fork in the road ahead. Ben decided to dodge the jeeps as he and Jill decided to fool them and lead them away. He and Jill were good drivers. Jill decided to play a trick on them as she got behind the jeeps, following Ben and the group. She used the sounds of guns firing to make Peter's men believe that she was firing at them from a distance.

The jeeps started swaying left and right on the road to avoid getting hit by the imaginary bullets, while Ben made sure to outrun them. Slowly, one by one, all the jeeps scattered and drove away to avoid getting shot while Jill cackled inside her van.

"They've been taken care of," Jill announced smugly.

The gang whooped and hollered while Ben thanked Jill for her genius trick. Soon, they came upon a bend in the road, and Ben chose that moment to stop and regroup. They all sat silently, observing the dark, silent road ahead of them while wondering what they were supposed to do next. Ben got out, knowing that no one would see him because he was still wearing camouflage, as the others remained in the van. They couldn't be sure that Peter's men wouldn't come back, so they were careful.

Ben's camouflage allowed him to remain hidden in the dark. Jill stopped the van near them as she caught up to them. She got out and approached Ben.

"Seems like your camouflage keeps saving us," Jill commented.

"You should get back inside," Ben said.

Jill noticed the stony expression on Ben's face and asked, "Are you regretting your decision to save the tiger and not shoot Peter?"

"I would never," Ben said. "I'm just pissed that he got away one more time. And now we don't even know where we are, or where we're going."

Ben ran his hands through his hair, hard and sticky due to the paint. He grimaced at the feel of dried paint in his hair, knowing how hard it would be to get out — if he ever managed to escape Peter, that is. Dana soon got out and joined the two standing by the roadside silently.

Jill thought about how her first impression of Ben was that he was just a sweet, nice guy. When she started getting to know him, her impression didn't change much, but she just started seeing Ben as the smart and passionate person he was. He could be driven when he wanted to be. Then, when he asked for her help with finding Peter, she realized that there was a side to the nice and sweet doctor that was much darker. It wasn't evil, no, but it was dark.

He could be vengeful and would do anything if it meant accomplishing his mission. Jill knew that by seeing how Ben was ready to kill Peter without hesitation. When he first said that, she had been shocked to her core. After all, he was a doctor. He was meant to save lives, not end them. Ben was also not a violent person, so it came as a shock to her that he would resort to such a thing for someone he hated. That was when she knew that Ben really had the worst time trying to recover from what Peter did. Otherwise, he wouldn't have been so cold and vicious in his treatment of Peter.

She knew that there was a very real possibility that Ben might just end up killing Peter by the time everything was over. Jill was smart enough to realize that. Although, she wasn't sure how she would respond to it. She had seen it first-hand how horrible of a person Peter was. His crimes definitely deserved punishment, but did he deserve to die? Was Ben the one who could give out a sentence on his life for his crimes? If it were the decision of a jury or the justice system, then it would be fine. It would be the people in authority who have the right to make such decisions.

Ben deciding that killing Peter was the only punishment fit for his crimes didn't sit well with Jill. He wasn't a judge or the jury. He couldn't give out a sentence on someone's life like that. He could justify it by saying Peter had murdered innocent beings, but did Ben have the right to decide? Jill could not justify it in her head. For her, it would be murder, not deserved punishment as Ben thought.

"What are we supposed to do?" she asked.

Ben shook his head and sighed, looking up at the dark sky as if a solution would present itself to him from the stars. "I guess we keep going until we hit the mainland," he said.

"What if we don't hit the mainland? What if we're going around in circles?" Jill thought.

"What do you mean?" Ben was confused.

Jill went back inside her van where she had set up shop. She came back a minute later, carrying a large map.

"So, I printed out the blueprint and map of Peter's compound," Jill said while showing the two the huge map.

Dana and Ben both peered over the map, not understanding what Jill was trying to say. She pointed out a gray area on the map, right behind Peter's compound, "I think this is where we are right now. Since it isn't marked up, I thought it was a lake or pond or something. But now I think it's this unmarked road in the middle of nowhere. And if that's the case, then we are technically still in Peter's territory."

Dana and Ben's eyes widened at that piece of information.

"You mean we haven't left the compound's boundaries?" Ben asked. "How do we get out?"

"That's what I am trying to figure out, but I don't see an exit anywhere nearby," Jill said, frustrated.

"So, we can't escape?" Dana asked incredulously.

"We can ... but we would have to go back the same way we came," Jill said hesitatingly.

"We can't do that!" Ben exclaimed. "They're probably lying there, waiting for us, and they will shoot us as soon as we make an appearance!"

"Do you have any other ideas then?" Jill raised an eyebrow. Ben was silenced. "Look, we have Stan and his men with us. They can provide us with cover. And we don't even have to go all the way back to the compound. We just have to connect back with this main road and then speed down the route till we connect back with the highway leading back to the mainland."

As they pondered over Jill's plan, Stan stepped out of the truck to join their discussion.

"What's going on? What's the plan of action?" he asked.

"We have to go back to Peter's compound in order to escape," Jill explained. She went on to explain the entire plan to Stan, and he seemed to agree with her.

"My men and I will provide backup, don't worry about that," he told Ben. "However, I do think that we need to be more careful and strategic. I think you should go first, Ben, and see how bad the situation is over there."

"That's suicide!" Jill argued.

"Ben is in camouflage. If he goes first, he can remain inconspicuous and gather intel for us to escape safely," Stan elaborated on his plan.

"I am in," Ben agreed immediately.

As they hashed out the plan and its details further, they stepped back in their respective vehicles and started the engine to return on the way they came from. The difference was that this time, Ben was driving the van, and Jill was driving the truck with the tiger. They knew that Peter's men would recognize the truck and immediately start attacking. So, Ben was supposed to go ahead before anyone and scope out the area for any potential threats. As the team headed out, Dana hoped that they would be able to escape easily, without any harm or danger.

Ben's ability to move silently and his camouflage were the biggest tools in their escape. They trusted him to accomplish the task without any signs of failure. Ben moved ahead and drove the truck toward the compound. As he got closer to the compound, he parked the van a few miles away from where it could be detected. He got out and crept closer to the boundary. He had his binoculars on and used them to observe the compound's perimeters.

He witnessed multiple men on alert and armed to the teeth, probably waiting to catch Ben. He knew that these men were aware Ben's group had nowhere to go but come back. They had them trapped because the only exit was through the compound. Ben stood to watch for a while, just observing the guards and waiting for the right time to go in undetected. He kept moving through the compound, remaining in the shadows and bushes so as not to get noticed. Ben was aware that the minute he got detected, they would open fire and gun him down. He had to make it out so his friends and the tiger could escape.

In the distance, Ben could see Peter standing with a bunch of his men, giving them orders and gesturing wildly with his hands. Ben felt his blood boil just at the sight of that man. Knowing how close he was, Ben had to restrain himself from shooting him right then and there. Peter was right within his grasp, yet Ben couldn't do anything. He kept watching him with anger filling his veins, the urge to incite violence on the vile creature making Ben tense. He clenched his fists and tried to count backwards so his anger could subside and he wouldn't end up making a stupid mistake. Ben prided himself on his restraint and cool head, but this was a true test of his patience.

As he watched, he radioed Stan to make his move. His men were supposed to create a diversion and distract Peter's men away from the entrance so that Ben and the others could move in and out silently without being caught. Two of Stan's men jumped over the compound's walls, and suddenly, there was chaos. Peter's men didn't waste a second before opening fire as they all ran after the intruders. Stan's men led them away from the entrance, and that was when Jill drove in with the truck. As silently as possible, she stopped the truck for a second so Ben could get on. Then she started driving out of the compound just as quietly as she had entered. They were meant to leave their van behind, so Stan's men had a way to escape, too, after they were done distracting the guards. While they fought with them near the opposite end, Jill drove the truck slowly out of the perimeters. They knew how close they were to being caught because the truck was visible for all to see.

While the guards were busy fighting with Stan's men, the group managed to escape in the truck along with the tiger. Ben noticed how hard they were fighting and turned his head away quickly when he noticed one of them getting shot. Soon, they were out of sight as Jill stepped on the gas and sped away.

"Should we wait for those guys to escape?" Jill asked Stan regarding his men who were back at the compound.

"No, that's not the plan. They know what to do, don't worry," Stan assured them all.

They were all tense as Jill drove away, not knowing how Stan's men were faring back at the compound without any help or backup. Having driven a few miles in the distance, they were startled when they saw a van tagging behind them.

Before anyone could get scared, though, Jill yelled, "That's our van! They made it!"

As Stan drove in the van behind the truck, everyone let out a sigh. They were beyond relieved that the guys made it out safely, knowing that without their help back at the compound, the team was as good as dead.

Stan radioed them, "Everything okay?"

"Yeah, boss. We good. Easy peasy, lemon squeezy," one of the men replied, making everyone chuckle.

"Thanks, guys," Ben radioed them, feeling utterly grateful, because they had saved their lives.

As the group celebrated the victory of their escape, Jill quieted them, "Now, who's going to navigate? I need to know where to go."

Dana unraveled the map, taking on the role of the navigator, "You need to go straight for five miles then turn left at the dirt road."

As Dana kept navigating her, Jill drove the truck. They were soon miles away from Peter's compound, heading toward the mainland. While coming there, they had taken a ferry to reach the highway that led to the compound. Peter's headquarters were very well-hidden from the reach of the general public and locals. It was on a secluded bit of island that was used mainly by fisheries. As Jill drove to the port, they all felt the tension leave their bodies.

They had managed to escape from the lion's den, no pun intended, without any injuries or fatalities. Without working as a team, they couldn't have managed to escape and release the tiger in Peter's captivity. They had all left that place with victory attached to their belts, a fact that surprised Ben internally. Not that he didn't trust his team or their efforts, Ben had been doubtful of their mission's success initially. Reaching the port, they all got out and stretched, because the stress of the entire night had made their muscles cramp up with tension. Just as the dawn's first light broke through the horizon, Ben and his team made their way to the port to look for a ferry or boat to help them get to the city. They had to be careful because they were carrying an exotic animal with them that they could allow nobody to find out about, or else they would be in trouble with the law.

Jill went to see if she could get tickets while the rest waited. Ben went to check up on the tiger to see if he was still unconscious and doing okay. He never turned off his veterinarian side, always being conscious about an animal's well-being and health. Since this was an endangered species and someone he had saved from the hands of dangerous people, Ben was extra cautious about its safety. In a few minutes, Jill came back with tickets to the next ferry, which was meant to leave in 20 minutes.

As the team waited to board the ferry, Ben and Stan made sure to keep an eye out to make sure Peter's men didn't follow them. They were bound to catch up any time now. Ben just hoped that they could leave without anything wrong. They were so close to getting away and saving the tiger. Then just as the truck was boarded on the ferry and it started to leave the port, Ben noticed several trucks and jeeps arriving in the distance. It was bright and early in the morning now, so the vehicles were very visible, and it was apparent that they were Peter's men. As the group breathed a final sigh of relief, the ferry departed, and they were officially out of the danger zone. Ben could feel his shoulders loosen up as he felt the weight being lifted off. He had not let himself hope for a positive outcome when they had initially set out for their mission the previous night. Yet, now that they were heading toward the city and away from Peter, after saving a tiger of all things, Ben couldn't have asked for a better outcome. He was immensely relieved and happy for having done it and grateful to his fellow teammates for helping him accomplish such a huge task.

He thought back to that safari and the nightmare that he had witnessed with his innocent eyes. Ben was aware that he hadn't truly recovered from the trauma of that incident. He knew that he was still harboring a lot of negative feelings because of that. He also knew that they would probably not go away on their own, and he would have to talk to an expert about it all. However, he also knew that after catching Peter and making sure his entire poaching ring was taken down, he would feel great. He had only stolen one tiger from him, and he already felt good about it. So, he knew that once he accomplished his goal of taking down Peter, he would feel a lot better about it.

When he was young and still suffering from the trauma of that incident, Ben's mother had told him something that he remembers till the present moment.

"Son, scars are like memories. The longer you stare at it, the more you hold onto them. If you stop acknowledging that they are there or simply distract yourself, they will fade away. You won't even see it, but they will heal and fade away in time as long as you don't keep scratching at it. Out of sight, out of mind."

Ben knew that she was just trying to help him cope with the trauma, but she was right. That was why he was determined never to forget what he saw. He would always keep bringing up that memory because he did not want to forget what happened.

It fueled his anger, hatred, and drive to get Peter to pay for everything he had done in his life. Those memories gave Ben a purpose, and remembering what happened just kept him going. Even though it was the most painful and upsetting memory he had, Ben wasn't going to not think about it. If he let those memories fade away, and if he let himself forget about why he was doing everything in the first place, then what would be the point? He had come so far in his journey. How could he let it all slip through his hands now? He couldn't, and that was that.

Ben could see the island getting further away from him and felt a sense of accomplishment. He hadn't managed to do much damage this time, but he did save the life of one tiger. That in itself was his biggest accomplishment. He managed to save one life from Peter's cruelty, and that was something that brought peace and happiness to Ben. He could feel his heart become lightened, with the weight of his subconscious being lifted off. He couldn't wait to save even more lives and innocent creatures from Peter's hands and bring them to safety. He wanted to give them all sanctuary as they deserved.

Did you know?

Tigers are illegally killed or poached because their pelts are valuable on the black market.

Chapter 10: Disbanded

Once the ferry took off with the group on board, along with the unconscious tiger in the truck, they all took a few moments to calm down and get their bearings in order. Yes, they had managed to escape and survive multiple attacks and dangerous situations, but the moment for celebration was gone. They were brought back to reality as the thought of heading back home hit each of them. Every single one of them was standing in different corners, silently stewing about the situation and what had occurred. Some of them had gone inside to rest after such a troublesome night. They were, understandably, exhausted.

Ben was probably the only one who felt a little relieved because he had managed to save an innocent life. It gave him the same feeling he got when he would operate on a serious patient and manage to save them. The relief and feeling of achievement always made him feel amazing. The others couldn't relate to that feeling too much. They weren't vets or anything close to that. Yes, they all wanted to save the poor animals from being slaughtered cruelly, but they wanted Peter. That was their main agenda and why they even came on the mission in the first place.

Ben turned to look at the others to see how they were faring, and he was met with frustrated and disappointed faces. He could tell that the others were not too happy with the outcome of their mission. They had basically gotten away with nothing, even though the tiger was saved. He understood how they felt; he wasn't too pleased either. Saving one animal was not going to do anything. Peter still had his business and could hunt more animals. He wasn't harmed in the slightest. Once upon a time, that would have been enough for Ben. He used to only care about the animals. However, something had changed within him over the years. The more cruelty he saw Peter dole out on animals across the world, the way he got away every single time and justice failed yet again, the more Ben lost his faith in the world and humanity. He was more than a little jaded by now.

The day he had first walked into his university campus, Ben was a wide-eyed, innocent, and hopeful young man. He still held faith in his heart regarding a lot of things. He was still someone who believed in the fact that, no matter what, people could change. You could change them simply by using the power of hope and faith and putting in some basic effort. That was the Ben of then.

The Ben of now believed that it was all complete bullshit. He didn't think that people could change so easily. He wasn't even sure if he believed that people could change at all. He had seen so much, been through so much, and wasn't in the right state of mind to actually have hope or faith. Peter kept evading him and getting saved as if the universe was playing some sick joke. Ben just wanted to catch the man and dole out some well-deserved justice, but the one person who should've been hit by some karma already was safe and secure. Ben sighed and went to wash himself off in the bathroom. He had to clean up and wash the paint, blood, and sweat off him. If he could, he would've scrubbed himself raw just so he could get rid of the ugly feeling he felt in his heart. He couldn't even talk to anyone about it, because everyone would just think of him as insane. After all, how could the kind, good doctor, Ben, turn into someone so violent and pessimistic? He treated puppies for a living, for Christ's sake.

As he washed himself at the sink of the bathroom, the door opened, and Stan walked in. They both looked at each other; then Ben went back to cleaning himself silently. Stan came to the sink right next to him and started doing the same. After splashing some water on his face, Stan finally spoke.

"I didn't want to say this back there," he started.

"Back where?" Ben asked in confusion.

"In front of Jill. I know she's ... sensitive to the talk of blood and violence," Stan said.

"Yeah," Ben sighed. "What did you have to say?"

"We have to bury someone," Stan said with a blank look on his face.

Ben froze. "Wait, what?! Bury who?" He was shocked. "I thought you said there were no casualties on our side."

"I said that not to raise any alarms," Stan said, continuing to wash.

Ben just stared at the man in disbelief. "It's one of the men I hired."

"A hired gunman?" Ben whispered.

"Yeah," Stan sighed. Then he started explaining what had happened.

***

"Boss! They're firing at us! We've been spotted!" the man said in his radio device.

"Hold tight! We're inside and scattered, but I am trying to find a way out! Do not get yourself killed, Geoffrey!" Stan yelled back through the radio.

Geoffrey could hear the chaos in the background, guns going off, men and women screaming in panic and pain.

"Boss, I can't hold them off much longer!" Geoffrey said from his perch high up on the tree. Before he could get Stan's response, the branch underneath him shook with a gunshot aimed right at it, and he was thrown off violently down the high vantage point.

"Ah, shit!" Geoffrey screamed as he landed right on his ankle. He could hear the bone break.

"Get up, you piece of shit!" a man in a mask screamed at him, pointing his rifle at him.

Geoffrey's sniper had fallen off along with him, but it was thrown to the side. He eyed it, but the shooter saw his gaze flicker to the side.

"Don't even think about it! Get the hell up!" he screamed.

Geoffrey knew he couldn't get to his gun on the broken ankle. The man would gun him down before he even took a breath. Suddenly, his radio crackled, and he heard Stan's voice.

"Geoffrey! Stay right there! Ben found a way out, I think, and we're coming out! Stay put! We're coming!"

Geoffrey looked at the radio then the man. He could either fight the man and wait for Stan and everyone else to come to rescue him, or he could admit the odds and give up. He knew he wouldn't last till the team showed up to rescue him. His odds were stacked as high as the tree he was on a few minutes ago.

"Who do you work for?!" the man screamed at him.

"I don't know, man. I was just hired for tonight, I swear," Geoffrey said with a sigh as he raised his hands in submission.

*"Don't f****** lie to me! Give me the name!" the man screamed.*

"I said, I don't know! I didn't get his name!" Geoffrey screamed back.

The man came forward and put the rifle to his head. "You give me the name now, or you die."

Geoffrey closed his eyes and thought about everything. He could give Stan up but then, what? He would die anyway. At least, he could still die with his honor intact. He thought of his beautiful wife, waiting for him at home, probably already asleep. They had been struggling financially, and when Geoffrey told her about his new gig, she was so happy. She didn't know what he did in reality; she just thought he did simple labor jobs. She didn't know that he was a gun-for-hire.

"I don't know," Geoffrey repeated as he opened his eyes.

However, soon, he heard someone calling his name.

"Geoffrey! Geoffrey!"

It was Robert! One of the men in Stan's team. He was saved! Geoffrey could've wept with relief. He might actually have.

"Looks like your friends found you, huh?" the man said in a mocking tone.

Just as Robert broke through the tree line, headed toward Geoffrey and the man holding him at gunpoint, the man tilted his head to the side and pulled the trigger.

Geoffrey only had enough time to widen his eyes and mutter, "No," before it was all done. The end.

Robert stumbled in his run, shocked by what he just saw. Then he started running even faster, shooting at the man with his rifle and screaming in anger. The man was dead in a matter of minutes, but he couldn't save Geoffrey.

***

Ben could only stare at the floor in numb shock. He couldn't feel anything. It was like the blood flowing through his veins had frozen. Even his thoughts had come to a halting stop. He could only think of the name of the man who had lost his life for them. A man he had never even met or seen. A man he had never even shaken hands with—Geoffrey.

"So, yeah," Stan cleared his throat. He looked away then back at Ben, "Robert took the body, but we have to bury him. I didn't want to do it back there 'cuz that's not his home."

Ben just nodded and whispered, "Yeah, okay, whatever you think is right. Just give him a proper burial."

Stan nodded, and Ben walked out. His feet felt like led, and his body felt numb. He was unfeeling from head to toe. He walked straight to the open bar, ordered himself a stiff drink, and tried to forget the entire nightmare of a night he had just spent.

***

The same evening, Ben was outside when he noticed Jill standing near the rails. He decided to walk over to Jill, since she was the only one who had actually joined him, not for any of her own reasoning. She simply wanted to help Ben achieve his noble goal.

"Hey there," Ben said, not knowing what to expect.

When Jill looked up with a tense frown on her face, he was shocked. Jill was the kind of person who was always cheery, fun-loving, and light of the room. Whenever there was a stressful environment at work, Jill would help cheer everyone up. She was the life of the party everywhere she went, sunshine in human form. So, it was more than shocking for Ben to see her so down and upset.

"Hey, what's wrong, Jill?" Ben asked worriedly.

"Are you seriously asking that?" Jill was incredulous. "After the night we just spent, you're asking me what's wrong?"

Ben was stumped for an answer.

"Everything is wrong!" Jill suddenly exploded, making everyone turn their heads to look at her. She kept going, though, "We were attacked! ATTACKED! By men with huge guns and a strong will to want to kill us all! And you! You were all too happy killing one of them! You're a doctor! You're supposed to be saving lives, not ending them!"

Ben could only stare at Jill in shock and a little bit of fear as she kept screaming.

"When you asked me for my help, I agreed wholeheartedly because I think you're a great person, doc. I look up to you. You're like the person with the most morals. Do you know why I started working for you? Even though that is not something, I expected to be doing. I had other offers from great IT companies, jobs that paid a lot more than being the technological expert at your clinic," Jill looked at Ben inquisitively.

He just stared back with confusion and shock written all over his face.

She brushed off her windblown hair and continued, "I wanted to work in your clinic because I saw how good you are. You are kind, sweet, and compassionate and have such a gentle way with animals that I couldn't say no to working with you. I never wanted to work for a corporation. I am also scared of violence and aggression, which is why I never went for an IT security company. You were my safest option!"

Ben could only feel guilt. He knew that Jill did not like aggressive situations. She was always anxious about it, telling him she couldn't even watch the news sometimes because it would be so intense. Ben knew all of that and still put her in such a dangerous situation, one where she handled herself so well and basically saved their butts.

"I agreed to help you because I didn't think you, of all people, would ever put me in danger. Now, I am scared for my life. And you're asking me what's wrong," Jill ended her little speech with a scoff and walked off.

Ben just stood there, staring at the spot where Jill was standing just a few seconds before. Dana wanted to approach and comfort him, but she wasn't sure how. She agreed with Jill in some ways. She had teamed up with Ben because she knew they both had the same goal, or at least that's what she thought. Dana came on this mission, endangered her life, and all for what? Her story was still not complete. She still hadn't caught Peter. What was she supposed to do now? Go back and report an unfinished story? A story that had no conclusion?

Dana was known for catching bad guys and putting them on public trial through her reports. This was the first time someone got away from her. She thought she could trust Ben not to let Peter get away, but he had, and now they were all left empty-handed. No matter how much she liked Ben, she couldn't help but blame him for it. Ben walked toward where Jill had gone to try to talk to her, maybe apologize, and Dana followed. She wanted to clear things up with him.

As Jill, Ben, and Dana talked, Ben listened to the frustrations of the women he had made a promise to.

"I'm not saying that saving that tiger wasn't worth it. I am so glad that we saved it, but I do feel like we could've accomplished a lot more tonight," Dana said to Ben as they stood in a shadowed corner.

Jill kept looking down, still a bit upset after her speech to Ben earlier.

"And, Jill? How do you feel?" Ben asked. After asking the same from Dana, he got the response that she wasn't too happy, because her report was now without a conclusion.

"You know how I feel. I don't think I need to elaborate on that further," Jill mumbled, still not looking up.

"Jill, you have to know how sorry I am. I honestly didn't think that it would get so bad tonight. I thought with my skills and your technical abilities, we would be able to get in and out without much trouble. It was only supposed to be a night to gather intel, that's it," Ben said to her. "But saving that tiger is not something I will ever regret, you know that. I'm just sorry that it put us all in so much danger."

Jill looked up, and her expression was sad, "I know you are. I am also happy that we saved the tiger. That is why I am here. To help you save those animals. However, I did not sign up to be shot at by criminals."

"I know, I know. I am really sorry, Jill," Ben said, with genuine regret in his voice.

Jill just nodded once and walked off. Ben knew she was still not okay, but he was willing to give her the space she needed to wrap her head around everything. Then he turned to Dana to solve her problems.

"I know you are frustrated, Dana, but we have got so much footage tonight. Isn't that helpful?" Ben asked, trying to help out as much as he could.

"All we have is the footage. What good is all this footage if we can't even catch that man while he was right there! You promised me that you wouldn't let anything stand in your way," Dana said.

"I know, but I had to save the tiger," Ben responded.

"You could've shot Peter and still got away with the tiger!" Dana shot back.

"I hesitated, okay? I wanted to; God knows how much I wanted to shoot him, Dana. Yet, I couldn't do it. I physically couldn't bring myself to shoot another person," Ben said softly. "I have lived my whole life according to the rule that violence and killing someone is not the answer. I hate that man more than anyone else on this planet, but he is still a living, breathing person. I save lives for a living! You have to understand that taking one had me a little hesitant."

Dana and Ben just looked at each other, not knowing what to do. They were both frustrated but unable to help the other.

"How about ... how about I go back and install some bugs back at his compound?" Ben started. "That way, whenever he makes plans, we would know, and then we could go after him."

Dana shook her head, "It's suicide going back there, Ben. I won't let you do it, no matter how much we need to catch that bastard."

"We have no other way," Ben argued.

"I don't care! I will not allow you to put yourself at risk just to get me my report!" Dana exclaimed.

Before Ben could say anything, a loud sound from the boat and the sudden shaking made them all stop. They grabbed the rails, not wanting to topple over as there was sudden chaos everywhere. People started getting back into their cars, exclaiming and shouting as they ran around in panic while the boat still creaked loudly and swayed in the water.

"Jesus Christ, what is happening?!" Ben yelled as he clutched the rails, with Dana right beside him.

As the boat creaked and rocked dangerously, people started yelling and fighting with the staff in frustration. Soon enough, the staff calmed everyone down by telling them they would dock soon. They had returned to the mainland instead of going the whole way through.

"Are you kidding me?! We just got away from there!" Stan yelled angrily.

The poor staff just looked at him, terrified and panicked, while Stan stared them down. He was already on edge since he lost touch with his men and didn't even get Peter during the process. Meanwhile, Ben just clutched onto the side of the ship, not wanting to lash out at the staff like Stan. They were trying their best, and it wasn't like it was their fault. Ben was still frustrated, though. He felt angry because this just set them back so many steps.

"Dammit," Ben cursed to himself. This was not what we needed right now.

"At least we didn't crash," Dana mumbled.

As the boat docked, everyone got out and clamored to find balance after being rocked on the boat so much. They were all frustrated when they heard the explanation by the ship's crew that there was some damage to the boat that made it unable to travel for the time being. They had to wait for the next ferry to arrive. Ben felt himself groan as he clenched his fists together. The group remained close in case any of Peter's men were still camped out near the harbor. They didn't spot any, though, and so they went to sit by a bench to decide their next course of action.

"We should just steal one of the private boats," Stan suggested angrily.

"That's not a solution!" Jill admonished as Stan just rolled his eyes.

"I don't think we need to do anything that rash. We can just camp out somewhere nearby since the next ferry will arrive tomorrow morning. We can't go anywhere else for the night," Ben said, trying to keep his calm, even though he could feel the anger churning in his stomach. He wanted to get back to the mainland as soon as possible, not wanting the tiger to wake up during their journey.

"Okay, but have you guys forgotten one huge, important detail? We have an unconscious tiger in the truck!" Dana exclaimed in whispers.

"Oh shit," Jill looked like she had just remembered that detail.

"I'll take care of it," Ben said tiredly.

They all turned to look at him in surprise.

"How are you going to do that?" Jill asked.

"I'll take the truck to the storage. I'll ask them to store it for me till the next ferry arrives and warn them I have precious cargo in the truck," Ben said.

"What if the tiger wakes up?" Stan posed the question.

"Even if the tiger wakes up during the night, it will be too sluggish or out of it to do anything. It was given a tranquilizer, and when the animal wakes up, it feels like a hangover more than anything. I'll leave some food for it in the truck, so it remains docile till we get to it in the morning," Ben explained.

They all agreed with the plan and dispersed to find camping equipment for the night. Soon enough, Stan found them a spot in the tree line near the harbor for them to camp, and they all headed toward the area. As they started to assemble their tents, Ben noticed how quiet it was among all of them. They seemed to be thinking about something, lost in their own thoughts.

"You know, David has a pregnant wife waiting for him back home?" Stan added after they had all settled down around a small bonfire.

David was one of the guys who had stayed behind at the compound while the rest got out. Thankfully, he had been able to get out and join them soon enough. Ben stared at the ground, not knowing what to do with the information.

"Eric has a blind sister who he keeps at a secret location so no one could get to her in order to harm him," Stan said.

Eric was the other guy who had fought Peter's men alongside David.

"Why are you telling us all this?" Ben asked in a quiet voice.

"I'm reminding you of the consequences should this have gone sideways. It's not just us here. It's our families and loved ones in danger, too," Stan said.

"You think I don't have a family? It's not like I have forced any of you to be here with me. This was your plan originally! Jill and I just tagged along!" Ben exclaimed.

The rest of the group stared in shock as the two men looked at each other, affronted.

"But you're the one who allowed it to go this far. If it were just my men and me like I had planned, Peter would be cold by now," Stan said, glaring at Ben.

"Do you want me to go back and shoot him? How many times do I have to explain myself? You're all acting as if I forgave Peter, shook hands with him, and then left. I had no choice at that moment! I would shoot him right in the eye if I had the option right now!" Ben yelled, standing up in his aggravated state.

Stan also stood up as the argument escalated. "You have to admit you're responsible! None of this would have happened if you didn't do what you did!"

Jill and Dana tried to stop the men from arguing further, but they refused to calm down.

"Fine! I admit! It was all my fault! Even the death of Geoffrey and your men shot are on me! Are you happy now?!" Ben exclaimed and then abruptly walked away.

Stan breathed rapidly, while Jill and Dana just looked at each other, lost in confusion as to what they should do. Dana was surprised to see Ben so worked up. Jill had rarely seen the doctor get so upset on a handful of occasions. They didn't know if they should have gone after Ben, so they remained where they were. After an hour or so, Dana tried to go after Ben, but Jill stopped her.

"Give him space. When he gets like this, it's better to leave him alone," Jill advised as she cleaned up the bonfire site and prepared to go to bed.

Stan and his men had already done that a long time ago. Dana sighed and walked off toward her camp, frustrated at how the group was in chaos, and the situation was nowhere near resolved.

***

Morning came, and the group woke up one by one, walking out from their tent in grumpy silence. They had barely gotten any sleep because of the tension of the situation. As Jill walked out, she looked around for Ben in her sleepy state.

"Where's Ben?" she asked in a sleepy mumble.

Before anyone could answer her, Ben suddenly walked toward them with his things in hand and looking ready to head out on the road.

"Everyone, get ready. We have to leave in ten," Ben said in a neutral tone, not looking at any of them, and then walked toward his tent.

They all stared at each other, not knowing how to handle the situation. As they all got ready and headed off toward the harbor to catch the ferry once more, Ben cleared his throat to address the rest.

"I know this mission didn't turn out to be the way you expected or wanted. I know you're all disappointed and frustrated, so there's no need to drag this out any longer. Once we get to the mainland, we'll go our separate ways. It was a bad idea to form this alliance. This way, we'll get to do our own thing, our way," Ben said with finality.

"But...," Dana tried to say something only to get interrupted by Ben.

"I have to get to the storage and retrieve the truck. You all get to the ferry," Ben said as he walked off toward the general direction of the storage.

They all stared at Ben's retreating in surprise. Nobody said a word, because they were all shocked at the turn of events. No one had been expecting this....

Chapter 11: Is It Enough?

As the sun rose high in the sky, the birds chirped, the city woke up gradually to start a new day, and children started making their way to schools. Ben woke up to the alarm blaring on his nightstand, which he turned off immediately. He had barely slept as it is. He sat up in bed and stretched, then sighed as he looked at the bright sun shining through his window. He went through his usual morning routine of taking a shower, shaving, brushing teeth, getting dressed, and then pouring himself a hot cup of coffee.

Ben poured out some food for his beloved puppy, who yapped at his ankles until he fed him. As he sat down to drink his coffee, he wondered how the day would be like for him. He looked at Silice, munching away on his breakfast happily, hoping he could get the same satisfaction from something so simple. Ben grabbed an apple after he was done with his coffee and made his way to the door to leave for work. He gave Silice pets, kisses, and rubs before tying his leash and leading him to the car.

Ben always dropped Silice off at a friend's place before going to work, so they could watch him for the day. He drove through the city, watching how people made their way to cafes before work and walked to the subway to commute to wherever they needed to be for the day. He used to love the morning hustle, watching all the people rush past and try to get to work on time. It was the mundaneness of the everyday routine that brought a kind of satisfaction to him. That morning, however, it couldn't stimulate Ben's mind enough. Everything seemed dull to him

THE POACHER'S ENEMY

that day. Ben greeted his staff of workers at the clinic as he arrived like he always did. He put away his things and put on fresh gloves to go meet some of his furry friends they kept at the clinic like he always did. Then he went to his desk and turned on the computer just as he always did. He tidied up his already clean desk like he always did. He looked at his desktop screen to check out his appointments and schedule for the day like always, but something was missing. His schedule was missing. He hung his head and sighed.

Of course, there was no schedule on his desktop. Jill always made it before leaving for the day, so the doctor could be informed as soon as he came in and turned on his computer. She always made sure things were organized, and Ben was always on schedule.

"Doc, the new guy is here," Jacob interrupted Ben's internal struggle, and he looked up.

"Sure, send him in," Ben said. He rubbed his face to try to at least look a little like the happy, kind vet he was perceived as.

The new guy walked into Ben's office and sat down in front of him. The two shook hands and greeted each other. Ben noticed how the new guy was a brunette, not a blond. He also didn't wear huge spectacles. He was also tall and lithe and seemed just like any other IT guy would.

"So, I take it you found your way here easily?" Ben asked, shaking off his thoughts.

"Yeah, I used the GPS," the new guy said.

It's not like Ben didn't know his name. He just couldn't stop referring to him as the new guy. It just didn't seem right to refer to him as "the new IT guy." Ben figured he still wasn't ready to accept the new reality. After they were done discussing the new guy's job and what it would entail, Ben gave him a brief orientation then faked an appointment to pawn him off on Jacob. He really wasn't in the right headspace to deal with new hiring that day or in the mood to be cheery or positive.

As the day went on, Ben worked quietly and treated his patients like he always did. However, it all felt different. It was the same job; some of the patients were usual too. So, why did Ben feel so different? It felt like somebody had taken his body and switched it. He felt like he was in the body of a different person, doing something that he wasn't familiar with. Being a vet and treating animals was the one thing he had always wanted to do. It was the one thing he was always focused on throughout his life. Then why was it not satisfying him anymore? Why did it feel lacking?

"Doc, you okay? You haven't even touched your sandwich," Jacob said through bites of his tuna sandwich. He had noticed that Ben had seemed zoned out the entire day. It seemed like he was present physically but not mentally.

Ben turned toward Jacob as if he had just noticed he was there and looked down at his plate. The sandwich he got was sitting at his plate, sad and cold. How long had he been staring in space for? Jacob thought.

"Sorry, Jacob. I must have a lot on my mind, I guess," Ben said.

"Don't apologize to me," Jacob said, and then after a pause, he continued. "Do you mind if I ask what's wrong? It's just that you don't seem like yourself today."

Ben feigned a smile and said, "I'm fine, Jake."

"Are you sure? 'Cuz if there's something bothering you, you can talk about it or take the day off. I know that not having Jill here must be making things difficult...," Jacob said hesitantly. He didn't know if he was allowed to discuss the topic of Jill just yet.

"No, no. I'm fine, I assure you," Ben said and started munching on his sandwich. He hoped that Jacob would let it go and not continue his line of questioning. Ben wasn't prepared to answer his questions.

Jacob just nodded and smiled, understanding that the doctor didn't want to talk about it.

***

"That's it? It was just because he was gassy?" The lady said incredulously.

"Yes, that's it. Don't worry about it. A lot of animals have that problem," Ben placated.

The lady seemed relieved as she hugged her pug to her chest, "Geez, Munchkin. You scared me!"

Ben chuckled and let the lady go on her way, amused at how many patients would come in just because their owners thought there was something wrong, but it was usually just a gastric problem. As Munchkin and her owner went away, Ben was officially done with the day. Even though it was only 3 p.m., he was done. His smile slipped off his face, and he went to sit at his desk. From his vantage point, he could see the new guy talking to some other employee, laughing and joking around. Ben raised an eyebrow as he noticed how the man was already adjusting to the workplace.

He decided not to be a creep and keep staring at the new employee, so he opened up solitaire on his computer. There was a time when Ben would see the morose and boring environment at his clinic and walk out to cheer his employees up himself. He would notice that the staff seemed down, bored, or just lacking motivation during the day, and he would try to make their days better. Sometimes, he would give them an early off if they didn't have any more appointments, only keeping one or two to stay with him for emergencies.

Ben was known to be a good and patient boss with everyone. He had curated a reputation for being kind, caring, and compassionate with all his employees. Even the people who came for interviews and didn't get the job would say only good things about Ben. The day Jacob came in for his interview, he wasn't too sure about the job. It was far from his home, and he had to make a long commute, but it was also the first good opportunity to come along in a long time. When Jacob walked in for his interview, he wasn't sure he would take the job if it was offered to him. He just could not handle the long commute. However, once he spoke with Ben and had a great interview, he was sure he didn't want to work anywhere else. He moved closer and made sure he didn't mess up the chance to get this job. Everyone loved working for Ben.

When Jill had joined the clinic, it was like things became even better. Ben was a great boss, but he couldn't be present at all times. Even though he was kind and friendly to everyone, he wasn't hyperenergetic and cheery like Jill. She uplifted the mood of everyone around her. They used to have a receptionist who was an older lady in her forties named Cindy. Cindy was like everyone's older sister and one of the most valuable employees Ben had. Not because of her level of work, but because of her personality and what she brought to the clinic. Everyone was sad when she told everyone she was moving to New York to be with her daughter who was about to give birth.

Jill, being Jill, threw her a huge farewell that was the biggest party Ben had ever thrown in his life. That was not even an exaggeration. Cindy was embarrassed but enjoyed the attention and care they showed her all the same.

Before leaving, Cindy told Ben, "Never let that one go."

"Who?" Ben was confused.

"Jill, of course! She's a gem and the day you lose her might as well be the day you shut this place down," she said candidly.

Ben chuckled, "Don't worry, Cindy. I won't let that happen."

Oh, how much he hated himself for letting it happen. Cindy would be so disappointed in him. As he looked around the clinic that day, Ben felt himself become despondent. He saw how everyone seemed dull and down, but he couldn't bring himself to cheer himself up. He just wasn't in such a good state of mind at the moment. So, he decided to hold himself up in his office until an appointment came. Then he would throw himself into his work until the day passed.

Ben wanted to distract himself. He had met with some clients, treated a few of his favorites, and even had a surgery scheduled for later, but he still didn't feel like he was mentally present. Nothing was able to get him motivated or feel productive. The work that used to bring him so much joy and satisfaction was doing nothing for him now. It wasn't like he didn't love those animals or care enough. He still cared, of course. Though, he just didn't feel as uplifted and motivated to work as usual. His friends, especially Jill, used to make fun of him for how he sought out work to decompress.

It wasn't his fault that Ben actually thought his job was fun. Other than the times he had to deal with some distressful situations, Ben always found a thrill in his work. It was why he worked so hard and focused so much during his academic years to become a veterinarian. Then he wondered that if Jill were there, would he have felt better? She always did manage to cheer him up. She was the bright energy in his workplace that always made working better for him. He loved having Jill working for him. Now that she had quit a while ago, he didn't know if he could just accept her lack of presence in the clinic.

The day after they came back home, Ben had come to work, dreading how Jill's mood would be. She remained quiet and reserved the entire day, but Ben figured that if he just gave her the space she needed, things would be fine soon enough. They worked together, so it wasn't possible for Jill to keep being upset, or else they would have serious problems. He hoped things would be better between them soon.

Ben considered Jill as one of his closest friends, so imagine his shock when Jill came in at the end of the day when everyone had left and Ben, too, was packing up his things to leave too. She quietly walked over to his desk. He thought she was going to talk to him so they could find a middle ground or resolve their conflict.

Nevertheless, she just handed him her resignation letter and said, "This is my notice. I can stay and train the new person you hire, but I am hoping you'd let me go as soon as possible."

Ben was shocked into silence. Had things really gone that far? Had he really hurt her that much? He couldn't believe what was happening. He tried to wrap his head around the fact the one person he trusted the most at work was leaving without any preamble.

"Jill...," Ben murmured. "Are you sure? I mean, I won't stop you if you want to leave, but I also don't want you to make any rash decisions just because you're mad at me."

"I'm not making a rash decision. I thought about this a lot, and I know this is what I want to do. I just...," Jill sighed. "I need a break. I need to step away and reevaluate things. You were an amazing boss and friend to me, something I will never forget. But I do have to move on now."

"You were an amazing friend and employee, too, Jill. In fact, I don't know how this place would function without you," Ben looked at the resignation letter once again, not knowing what else to say.

"Well, do you accept it?" Jill asked.

"I mean, if this is what you want to do, then I won't stand in your way," Ben responded.

That was the last day he saw Jill and also the last day that they spoke to each other. Ben had let her go without a fight or argument because he wasn't the kind of person to force someone to stay by his side if it didn't make them comfortable. Jill was obviously shaken by the whole ordeal, and maybe stepping away was the right thing to do. Ben knew that he couldn't step away from that, though. He was attached for life. It was all he knew, and he wouldn't give up on his goal so easily.

Even Ben could feel the changes in him after what happened. They had only been gone one night, but everything they faced, including almost dying multiple times, did make him pause. He was not abandoning his mission, but he had suffered a huge blow, to say the least. Ben wasn't sure if he could even continue doing what he wanted to do without the help of Jill, Dana, and Stan's team. It was because of them and their teamwork that they were able to even get so far. After coming home, the first thing that Ben did was take the tiger to his clinic to examine it thoroughly. He wanted to make sure the tiger hadn't been hurt or gotten injured during the whole ordeal. After examining it, Ben concluded that the tiger was healthy, if not a little scared and feral. He called his friends in the industry to make sure it would be taken somewhere safe. One of his friends from a sanctuary came and collected the tiger in the morning, Ben having stayed with it in the clinic the entire night.

Once Ben was sure that the tiger was safe and sound and far away from Peter's clutches, he was finally able to go home and sleep. Even though he was exhausted beyond belief, Ben couldn't sleep that night. He couldn't stop thinking about what had happened. He felt the effects of the adrenaline rush wear off slowly, leaving him tired, scared, and shaken. Ben hadn't lived a life of thrill and adventure. He had definitely never been in near-death scenarios, at least.

He thought about the others. Jill was still pretty upset with Ben, which was understandable. She wasn't a fan of violence, and the situation they had been through was traumatizing enough. Dana was upset because her report didn't get the conclusion she wanted, and she was forced to let go of it for the time being. Ben thought he knew Dana enough to know that she wouldn't abandon the story altogether, but just put it away for now just until she could get Peter.

Stan and his men were quiet on the way back home, quickly separating and driving off wherever they wanted to after they all reached the city. Ben understood that too. Stan was a man of action. He couldn't have understood Ben's emotional reasoning. Stan had gone in with one goal in mind, and Ben had jeopardized that. Since he was a militant, Stan was obviously not happy with the fact that their mission had been a bust, especially after he almost lost two of his men and one of them couldn't make it. Ben could tell that their group dynamics were strong. Stan cared about the men who worked with him, never thinking of them as collateral.

Ben harbored a lot of guilt for that night—guilt that was eating away at him. Usually, when he was bothered, he would talk to Jill. She could always get him to stop overthinking or being too lost in his thoughts. Now, she wasn't there anymore. Ben looked over at the new guy sitting in Jill's place and felt regret. He had lost such a good friend due to one night of impulsive decisions. Ben hoped that one day, even if it was years ahead, Jill would be able to forgive him, and they could mend their friendship. He stood up and walked over to the new guy, intending to make an effort to at least be nice to him.

"So, Kevin, how's it going? Hope we haven't given you too much trouble for the first day," Ben said amicably.

"No, sir. It's been fun to meet everyone and help them out," Kevin said with a genuine smile.

"You can call me Ben, it's okay. I don't really see myself as a 'sir,'" Ben said.

Kevin chuckled and nodded, "Of course, si- Ben! I mean Ben!"

Ben chuckled and stayed to talk to the guy more. Kevin was in his early twenties, and sure, he wasn't a bubbly, intelligent blonde girl. He was still a smart and good guy. Ben could tell that he was shy and not used to such an active workplace. At least he seemed to like the animals. As the day wrapped up, Ben was still not high in spirits, but he hoped the next day would be better. He cleaned his desk and got ready to leave. He drove by his friend's place to collect Silice, who immediately pounced on him in greeting.

As Ben let Silice try to kill him with licks and excited barks, he felt a bit better. Silice was someone he hadn't disappointed. He neither had hurt him nor broken any promises. Silice still liked him. Later that evening, after Ben got home from walking Silice, he sat down on his couch to catch up on some news and have his dinner. He knew that his life wasn't too exciting, but he liked it like that. He liked coming home to his dog, making his dinner, and then eating it in silence while he watched some TV.

Ben was watching a news channel while having his spaghetti dinner when he was startled. The images on the screen showed a shootout between some gangs, and the violent imagery was much too familiar to Ben. He immediately turned the TV off, panting and feeling his heart beating loud and fast. He felt cold sweat running down his brow as he shivered a little. He had goosebumps on his arms and neck. His dinner was completely forgotten on the table in front of him as he tried to get himself in order. His breathing and heartbeat were rapid, his muscles tense.

With strength he didn't even know he had, Ben tried to calm himself down. He knew he was panicking, but he had to control it before he got a full-blown panic attack. Silice jumped up on the couch, probably able to tell that Ben was not okay. He started licking Ben's face, and he had to admit that it helped. Ben petted Silice while trying to keep himself calm.

"What the hell?" Ben mumbled to himself.

Silice barked as if replying to him, and Ben smiled to himself. At least he had Silice. Ben decided that he had had enough of this day, so he prepared to go to bed. After washing the dishes, giving some food to Silice, and changing into his pajamas, Ben slipped into his bed. He lay there, staring up at the ceiling, the only sound being the ticking of the clock and the slight hum of the air conditioner. He felt the heaviness of sleep in his eyes, but they weren't closing. He was tired and had to wake up early for work, but he couldn't shut off his brain.

The images on the TV earlier had reminded him of the night they were at the compound. The night he let Peter go. For Ben, it was all too much. He didn't know what messed up the part he should focus on. The fact that Peter got away, how a man had died for their mission, the fact that they all could've died, how he lost one of his best friends because of the tension, the way he lost sight of the mission itself, or the fact that he couldn't even fulfill the promise that he had made to Dana.

As he turned to his side, he remembered the moment a man had found him, and he was almost shot. They were running through the maze that was the compound on the inside. Ben tried to find a way out. He was with Stan, but they had gotten separated. As Ben made his way through the maze of hallways, everything had been so loud. There were sounds of people screaming in pain, anger, and panic. Then there was the cacophony of bullets being fired, even smoke bombs going off somewhere, the grunts and shouts of people being hurt, and the thundering footsteps as everyone ran around, trying to get out.

Just as Ben had turned a corner, he was met with the face of someone he didn't know. He looked older, with gray hair that was a mess. His face was marred with wrinkles and scars, making him look scary and intimidating. He was also huge, almost looking like a wall next to lanky Ben. Ben wasn't skinny, he was strong enough to know Krav Maga, but he didn't have bulky muscles.

Before Ben could react, the guy had a gun pressed to his forehead. Ben stayed frozen, letting the guy think he had the upper hand. Then he suddenly reached out to kick him in the stomach while also striking at his throat at the same time. The guy keeled over in pain, and Ben took the chance to kick at his bent knees, sending him sprawling back on the floor. The gun was shaken from his hand and thrown to the side. The man looked up at Ben with shock, and then panic filled his eyes immediately.

"Please ... don't kill. I let you go. You can run. I let you go," the man said in broken English with a thick Russian accent.

Yet, Ben didn't have time to reach for the gun before the man was shot right between the eyes. Ben gasped, turned around, and met with the sight of Stan with a gun held up. He lowered his gun and said, "One less on your conscience. You're welcome."

Ben just stared at him and said, "I had it."

"I just made it quicker," Stan shrugged.

Stan moved past the dead Russian man, and Ben followed behind him, trying not to think of all the death that surrounded them.

That night had left a lot of scars on Ben's mentality, but the deaths were the hardest to deal with. He didn't know if he would ever recover from the trauma of it all. Even if they were working with Peter, did they deserve to die? Weren't they just like Geoffrey, hired guns? Who was to say who deserved to die or not? Those people were just following orders. They probably also had families, friends, and a life outside of that compound. Didn't they deserve to go back to all that? Ben let that philosophical dilemma keep him up even longer.

After an hour or so, Ben finally managed to go to sleep. He remained in a deep sleep for a few blissful hours until he suddenly woke up. He sat up in bed and panted, his entire body soaked with sweat. His heart was racing, and his vision was blurry. He tried to look for his phone to check the time, and when he did, he squinted at the bright screen. The digits blinking up at him told him it was 3:16 a.m. Ben got out of bed to go get a glass of water. He also went to the bathroom to splash some water on his face.

Ben had had a nightmare, which made him wake up in a cold sweat. He couldn't even remember what the dream was, but it was terrifying. He was still shaking a bit, so he decided to get a hot shower to relax his muscles and because he was sweating so much. After his shower and lots of glasses of cold water, he was finally calm. He climbed back into his bed, but he knew he couldn't go back to sleep. He decided to play around on his phone for a bit, then went to his secret room. He hadn't been back there in a long time.

The last time he was inside that room, it was with Jill and Dana as they planned for the mission to storm Peter's compound. If only he had known then what he knew now. They do say that hindsight is twenty-twenty. As Ben sat staring at his wall of clues and signs connecting to Peter, he realized he had put too much work into focusing on Peter and not on his team. They were all a team. They had bonded as a team quickly. He felt so bad about what happened that he couldn't get it out of his head.

When he came back to bed, Ben looked at his phone for a while. He was indecisive until he decided to be impulsive and call the person he was thinking about. He went in his contacts, pulled up "Dana," and slid his finger to place a call. The phone rang, and Ben could feel his anxiety increase with every passing second. His leg shook, and he was almost about to hang up when suddenly the call was answered.

"Um, hi, Dana? It's Ben. Um, I know you were probably asleep, and I am disturbing you, but I just really wanted to talk to you about-," Ben started rambling when he got interrupted by a voice that was not Dana's.

"Oh, hello, Ben! I was looking forward to talking to you!" Peter's grating voice and laugh hit Ben's ears like nails on a chalkboard, and he was shocked into silence.

Ben pulled the phone away from his ear to check if he really had dialed Dana's number.

Why is Peter picking up Dana's phone? Where's Dana?

Chapter 12: The Poaching Party

As soon as he heard Peter's annoying voice from the other hand, Ben felt his eyes go wide and face pale. He clutched the phone in his hand in a tight grip, almost to the point of breaking it. Clenching his jaw, he felt the red-hot anger boiling up inside him.

"Where's Dana? What have you done to her?" Ben asked with barely restrained fury in his voice. He wasn't usually a furious, aggressive, and violent kind of guy, but in this situation, he couldn't help but feel the cold grip of rage grip his heart and squeeze until he felt his heartbeat slow and the need for vengeance fill his body.

Funnily enough, it reminded him of his very first serious relationship in life. Ben and Dana were not dating. They weren't ever even close to it. However, the situation reminded him a lot of Karen. When Ben was in his first year of vet school, he had met a girl. It wasn't that Ben had never been in a relationship before then. Of course, he had. He had a few relationships in high school, yet they were never as serious as this one with Karen. He was always too focused and distracted by his academic goals to ever really entertain the idea of a fully committed relationship.

The girls he dated not very often were more than upset by his lack of effort into crafting and establishing a relationship. Sometimes, they thought he was cheating on them, and other times, they thought he was simply not serious about them. In reality, though, Ben was just not interested in having something too serious, because it would take him away from his goals. This is why when he started dating Karen, he was surprised by how much he actually liked her. She was funny, quirky, and attractive. Ben didn't think he was ready for a serious relationship, but he was willing to work with Karen.

She was someone who understood his shortcomings and the fact that he had specific goals in mind that he would rather spend time and energy on than his social life. However, Ben still had his issues with commitment and relationships, so he started spending more time in the library than on dates with his girlfriend when the time came for final exams. Sometimes, he would even forget that they had plans together until he would get a call from a very pissed-off Karen.

Since Ben was so unaware of his issues and the decline of his relationship, it came as a shock to him when Karen broke up with him. Her reason, though, made complete sense.

"Ben," Karen sighed as they sat on the ragged couch in her little apartment off-campus. "I don't know how to tell you this...."

"What is it?" Ben asked.

Karen looked up at him. Her eyes were filled with tears of guilt and sadness. "There's someone else...."

"What?!" Ben was shocked to his core. "What do you mean?"

Then Karen proceeded to tell him how his absence had created a hole in their relationship. A gap that some guy in Karen's class filled.

"Every time you ditched me or flaked out on our dates, he was there for me. He would bring ice cream, pizza, whatever I needed at the time to make me feel better. You weren't there. He was," Karen cried.

Ben didn't know what to say to that, so he just remained quiet.

"You're not even gonna say anything?" Karen asked.

Ben remained quiet.

"No screaming? Cursing? Why aren't you upset?!" Karen yelled desperately.

"Because I don't know what to say," Ben told her calmly. "I understand. I wasn't there for you and he was. You deserve better than the way I've treated you. If you want to go, then I'm not gonna stop you."

"So you're just giving up? You're not even gonna fight for me? For us?" Karen seemed angry and hurt.

Ben just remained silent. It wasn't that he wasn't sad or upset, but he realized that it was a fight he had already lost. That day, when Karen broke up with him, she said something that shook him to his core.

"You're never gonna be able to sustain relationships like this, Ben. You have to open up and let people in. You can't just course through life with no attachment to anything. If you don't fight for the people that you care about, you're gonna be alone forever."

At that moment, as he considered the fact that Dana was in probable danger, Ben was willing to fight. He wasn't the same Ben anymore. The Ben who let things happen to him and just smiled through his pain. The Ben who let people walk in and out of his life without any consequences. He was the Ben who was going to fight and fight hard for the things and people he cared about. For once, he was not going to give up. Not without a fight.

There was also the fact that Peter was the one person in the whole world who could make Ben murderous. He was ready to let go of all his values, ethics, and moral compass just so he could get his revenge and end Peter. Peter had the ability to bring out the worst and extreme sides of Ben that not many people had got to witness. He had a vengeful, dark side that he didn't like showing to others. However, Peter always managed to trigger that part of him, and Ben couldn't help it.

"Now, why would you think I did something? Dana is right here! She's doing absolutely fine, too," Peter said in a friendly manner as if he and Ben were the oldest of buddies, simply discussing friendly things.

This man was truly a psychopath if he could act like this with someone who was trying to ruin him. Ben was sure of it, and that made his anger flare up even more. He tried not to think about Dana and what kind of condition she could be in at the moment if Peter was the one answering her phone. It made him scared, and that was an emotion he didn't like. He had never felt scared when it came to Peter. Nevertheless, Ben also didn't want to do something stupid, especially because Dana's life was in danger.

"Listen, you bastard, I am only gonna say this once, and I want you to listen carefully. You hurt a hair on Dana's head, and I will make sure you cease to exist. I don't give a shit who you are, what kind of power you have, or how many guns you own. I will hunt you down. That's a promise," Ben threatened Peter.

"Aw, Ben! I'm actually scared now! I'm literally shivering right now!" Peter said in mock fear, followed by his shrill laughter, and hung up the phone.

Ben clutched the phone for a moment, wondering if it would be too difficult to get a new one if he broke it. After a few seconds, he decided not to risk it and immediately got up to prepare. Now he really couldn't sleep. His mind was filled with images after images of Dana being caught and held in a place similar to dungeons that he saw in Peter's compound. Ben could not sit around, knowing that Dana was in danger. He had to find her, and he had to do that fast.

Ben went into his secret room, pushed a button underneath the desk, and a large safe opened up in the wall on the side. It was a secret compartment where he had hidden his weapons and other gear. He had not made it known to anyone, not even during the mission when the whole team was together. Ben only kept this safe as a last resort. He didn't think this very mission would come down to this. As the safe opened up, Ben perused the armory he had built. The day he decided he was going to go after Peter and end his entire poaching ring, Ben knew he needed reinforcements. Without such aid, he couldn't even hope to get close to Peter. The last time he got close to him was when their mission was mainly carried out using weapons such as these. Ben knew they were necessary for this mission as well. He had to rescue Dana.

Ben started preparing, packing away the weapons, equipment, and things that he would need. He packed his camping equipment, camouflage gear, and other tools he would need to go after Peter. After Ben was all packed, he left a message for Jacob, telling him he had to take sick leave from work. With his attitude the day before, Ben was sure Jacob would understand his need to take a day off work. Soon, Ben was on the road, driving his jeep as fast as possible toward the place he thought Dana was kept — the same jungle he had been in with the rest of the team.

Ben was going back to the jungle to find Peter because he knew that Peter was like a rat. The man would always hide in the jungle when he did something wrong or illegal, which was always. That was why he had built his compound in such a remote location, surrounded by the jungle and not a human to be found nearby who wasn't working for him. Ben was looking forward to meeting Peter again. He could finally take out his frustration and anger for what had happened the last time. After arriving in the jungle, Ben set up his camp and proceeded to observe the place for any trails, tracks, or signs of Peter. He put on his camouflage got up and went around the area where he felt he could see some signs of recent activity. It was a lesser-known fact about him, but Ben was really good at tracking. He was able to find clues and tracks where people couldn't see anything. In his camouflage, it made it easier for him to fly under the radar. After a while of not finding any signs of Peter, he took a break near his campsite.

Ben had disguised his camp to give an impression as if a hunter was camping there, nothing too suspicious if Peter or his men did stumble across it. He was taking a five-minute break from his search, but his senses were still alert and sharp. He was waiting to hear or see any signs that could point toward Peter's presence. Ben was sure he would come here; he had no doubts about it. He had always observed the jungle before poaching season.

While he sat and waited for any obscure move or sound in his vicinity, Ben was forced to think back of the last time he was there — the last time he had been with his team of friends and comrades who had joined in on his noble battle against Peter. They were willing to band together and put their lives in danger for his mission. He couldn't have been more grateful. However, things had not turned out the way that they had hoped or planned them to. They hadn't experienced the worst-case scenario that Ben thought of, but it was still very brutal.

Ben had known the risks of coming on such a mission. He knew that there were lives at stake, the entire mission was at stake, and he also knew that if anything bad were to happen to any one of them, he would never be able to live with himself afterward. For him, things had to go smoothly. There was no other option. Yet, when everything went sideways, he still held hope that they would somehow make it through as a team. He was letting all the weird thoughts grow deeper.

He had realized how wrong he was. Not every one of them had been working toward such a mission their whole lives. Sure, Dana was used to investigating criminals and putting them away, but even she was not prepared to literally go to battle with one of the worst people out there. Ben had been thinking of them along the same lines as him. That they were just as equipped and prepared as he was, though that was not the case. For them, it was all very intimidating and scary. Jill, especially, was not prepared for a mission like that, but she came along only because she was such a good and kind-hearted friend. Yet, that had cost them their friendship, and Ben could not have been more devastated.

That was when he knew that he had overestimated not them but himself. He thought he was enough for the mission and that they wouldn't even have to do much. That he would be able to get them to Peter's compound, fight him and his men, rescue the animals, get Peter to jail, and then bring them all back safe and sound. That was very foolish of him. If he only hadn't been so shortsighted, he could've stopped his friends from coming on a mission that was doomed to fail or at least prepared them well enough in advance so that things wouldn't go too bad if he was indisposed. Throughout their mission, Ben had refused to think about any of them or how they felt. He was so focused on his vengeance and thirst for Peter's blood on his hands that he had let his friends become cannon fodder. He was willing to let them sacrifice themselves, and yet, at the end of it, he didn't even appreciate all that they had done and were willing to do for him. If he had just stopped to think for a minute, he could have prevented a lot of the things that went wrong. Ben realized that he should never have asked anyone to join him in the first place. He should've come to Peter's compound alone as he had originally planned. In that way, he would've been able to keep everyone safe.

He wouldn't have lost Jill's precious friendship and respect, Stan wouldn't have lost a man on his team, and Dana wouldn't have lost the one criminal whom she wanted to get. Yes, Ben blamed himself for all of it. Why shouldn't he? After all, they were all there because of him. If it hadn't been for him, none of them would've been there that night. Before he could sulk any further, suddenly Ben heard what sounded like a person mumbling very far away. He had become attuned to the usual sounds of the jungle for quite a bit, so when a human spoke, it immediately alerted him.

Ben quickly got up and followed the direction where the voice was coming from stealthily. He was hoping it was Peter, but he would be really pissed if it was just a hunter or hiker. He followed the voice until he could get close enough to hear snippets of what they were saying. Apparently, there were a few. Ben was extra careful with making sure that nobody could hear him while he sneaked up on the group, tracking through the jungle, unaware that they were being watched. Getting close enough, he hid behind a tree, low on his stomach, to observe the men who were walking by and talking among themselves.

"I don't know, man; it doesn't seem like she believes me," one man said.

"She would when you bring home the bread," the other replied.

"But how can she not trust me? She's met Peter! She knows I work with him on-site!" The first guy said, frustrated.

Ben didn't care what they were talking about since he just found out that they worked for Peter. He was just biding time to make sure that when he attacked, he had the upper hand. There were three men in total. Ben observed his vantage point and decided to take out the one in the back since he was barely speaking and could go unnoticed.

Ben took out his blowgun and tranquilizer-laced darts to take out his targets one by one. He blew, and, within a second, the man walking a few paces behind the two guys talking fell down. Ben had timed it well, such that when the man would fall, he would fall on top of the bed of leaves that would soften the impact and not alert the rest about their partner falling unconscious.

Then before Ben could blow at his next target, he pulled out his Glock 19 with the silencer on and held it in his other hand. Soon, he had the other guy unconscious, too, and the first guy was completely taken aback. Ben jumped up to run at the man left and attacked him from behind while he stood staring at the unconscious bodies of his partners, trying to figure out what had happened. Ben silently put his gun to the man's head, and he was still immediately, recognizing that he couldn't do much at the moment. However, before Ben could ask the man anything about Peter, he suddenly maneuvered in a way that he twisted his body and escaped Ben's hold.

Ben's shock allowed the man the time to punch Ben and send him reeling back into the tree behind. Ben responded with a hit of his own, and the two started to tumble on the jungle floor. Ben's gun was knocked out of his hand, and he was left to use hand-to-hand combat skills to try to underhand the other guy. The guy was also a skilled fighter, and he was not letting Ben get the upper hand. In a few minutes, Ben was on his back with the man on top of him and punching him in the face. His hands and knees were locked by the guy. He was choking Ben. He knew he had to do something fast, or he would lose consciousness and the leverage he had gotten.

Ben spotted his gun lying just within his reach on the ground, and he knew he had won. He reached out for the gun and instantly whipped the guy in the face with it. He tumbled off Ben and fell down on the floor unceremoniously, having gone unconscious. Ben stood up, panting and wiping the blood from his mouth. He had wounds all over—bruises and cuts from the punches that man had managed to get in. Ben moved along and started to search the man's bag for items that could point toward the location where Peter was keeping Dana. Suddenly, one man on the ground groaned and started shuffling around.

Ben quickly went to him and grabbed him by his throat to yell in his face, "Where is he?! Where is he keeping Dana?!"

The man winced and groaned, responding, "I don't know what you're talking about!"

He coughed, and Ben shook him again. "Tell me where Peter is!"

"The compound, man! The compound! Shit," the man groaned again and lay back down.

Ben disregarded him and immediately went to pack up his things and head to the compound. It would take him hours to reach the place, and he had to hurry. After hours spent driving and then catching a ferry to get to Peter's compound, the anger was still boiling up inside him. He was going to find him and make sure he regretted his decisions. It was nighttime when Ben finally managed to reach Peter's compound. However, as opposed to the last time that he was there, Ben found something odd.

The entire place was silent. The only sound that surrounded him was the chirping of crickets and nothing else. Ben sneaked inside and was shocked to find the perimeter unguarded. Peter always had his men standing guard, so where were they? He ran through the compound's grassy yard and found it completely empty — no huge scary men with guns in hand every few feet inside the compound. The lights were off, and the place looked abandoned. Just to make sure, Ben decided to sneak inside and see if it truly was as empty as it looked. He went through the front door, not the secret door to the basement like he had the previous time. After he walked in like he was just visiting a friend's house, Ben was even more shocked. The place was blanketed in darkness, and there was no soul to be found. It was deathly quiet, and it unsettled Ben. The whole place was turned upside down, as if they had left in a rush, trying to gather as much as they could in a short time. Ben walked throughout the compound, every room and hidden passage that he hadn't even seen the last time, yet there was no one and nothing. It looked like the place had been abandoned for years, not a couple of days.

Ben ran down to the basement where the dungeons in which Peter kept the animals were. He was a bit relieved but also angry to see that there was no animals. Peter had obviously vacated the premises in a hurry as if he knew Ben was coming. That was the only thing that Ben could figure out. He had no idea what other explanations there were for the current situation. Stumped, Ben left the compound and went to the port, because that was the only place where he could find people. The locals were fishermen who came just to catch fish on the little island.

As a last resort, Ben decided to question the locals on what they had seen or heard. Surely someone must have noticed something if Peter's entire gang had vacated the premises altogether. He was hoping that someone could help shed light on what happened in the time before Ben came. He talked to a few people, some not even willing to speak to him for some reason. From his observation, he figured out that the people weren't too keen on talking about what happened on this island. They appeared to be scared of Peter, almost as if Peter was doing them a favor by letting them come to the island and work on it.

Ben understood how people didn't want to be involved in anything to do with Peter. The poor villagers feared for their lives and livelihoods. As Ben talked to a few people who actually wanted to talk to him, he figured out that they had all left during the night. That was why not a lot of people got to see them leave. Leaving in the dead of night only confirmed the suspicions in Ben's mind. They were carrying out something that couldn't be witnessed by anyone else. As he was talking to one of the locals, the man happened to mention a guy he had spoken to the previous night.

"I was one of three men still here last night. We were just wrapping up when one of them came to ask me if they could borrow our boat. He didn't look like a fisherman, so I asked what he needed it for. The man pulled a gun on me! But the boss-looking man behind him stopped him, and they just took another bigger boat," the man explained.

"Can you tell me what they looked like?" Ben asked eagerly.

"The one who threatened me was an Indian-looking guy. I think his name was 'Rahul' or something. The rest of them were your typical white and black thugs," the man said, grunting in annoyance.

"And can you tell me where they were headed?" Ben asked again.

"I think the boss mentioned something like the 'city HQ' or something," the man said.

"Thank you, sir," Ben said and rushed to catch the next ferry. Ben knew of only one location in the city that could be it. He wasn't sure, but it was the only lead he had.

During his time researching with Jill, she had managed to find one other location where Peter used to operate from before building and moving to the compound. Once again, he found himself thanking God for having met Jill in his life. Without her, he wouldn't have been able to come so far.

During the ferry ride to the mainland, all Ben could think about was Dana, helpless and scared, locked away in some dark basement. Rationally, he knew that Dana was not a damsel in distress, but he couldn't help but fear for her. She was strong, no doubt, but Peter was a psychopath. He couldn't be trusted. She could be in serious danger. After reaching the mainland, Ben's first order of business was to wash off the camouflage and find this Rahul guy who apparently worked with Peter.

Jill had been able to find that there was another location, but they never could pin down the address of the place. She just found out about it because Peter had two properties in his name, and one of them was the compound. Also, the fact that the first property was supposedly the one he bought right after his poaching business took off. All Ben had to do now was find Rahul and get him to spill the address. He went back home and fired up his computer.

Before they had gone on their mission, Jill had upgraded and installed a new system for Ben, saying it was for him to carry out small tasks on his own if necessary. It also disgusted her that he was still using Windows 7. As he used the very fast and accurate computer to locate Rahul, he found himself thanking Jill for her amazing mind. The tracker she installed was able to track the account transactions of Peter. While using it, the system would ping upon detecting the location, and you could then get access to the security camera footage of that area to see where Peter was or what he was doing.

Ben figured that if Rahul was with Peter when he would use his card, he could find him. Peter would be found as well. Suddenly, there was a ping, and Ben zoomed in on the location. It was near a café, and he could only see one man carrying a cup of coffee, walking away. The man definitely looked Indian. Ben noted down his car plate number as Rahul got in a car and sped off. Then Ben used Jill's system to find the car with that number.

Ben was successful in finding Rahul. He was hanging out near an alley, smoking up in his car, and there was no one around. Ben immediately got to the car and threatened Rahul to open the door. Rahul got scared, thinking it was some robber. Then Ben started asking him questions regarding Peter.

"Oh, man. Why does this always happen to me?" Rahul groaned, thinking about the woman who had caught him and said similar things. "Look, I am only working for Peter till I can pay off my student loans. I have no loyalty to that man."

Ben smirked and said, "Then it shouldn't be a problem if you told me where he was."

Ben kept asking questions, and Rahul answered them honestly one by one. He knew he was stuck, and there was no other way he could escape. Peter was not worth risking his life for.

"You're quite the loyal follower," Ben remarked sarcastically.

"You want the info or not?" Rahul scowled.

Rahul started ranting off about the location and what Peter was up to.

"That's where he's working from nowadays?" Ben asked.

"Yeah, the location is perfect for him. Plus, the hotel signs an NDA so no one can snitch on Peter if they see anything suspicious," Rahul explained.

"What else?" Ben dug deeper. He knew this was the only chance he had to gain some valuable information about Peter.

"Well, he's also planning a party. A huge poaching party, that is," Rahul rolled his eyes. "He's got everyone running errands for it. Apparently, some important guests are coming."

"What guests?"

"Friends and contacts of Peter. Other poachers who run a similar ring. They will all get together and have a huge poaching party. Peter's going all out," Rahul said.

Ben was shocked. *How low could this man stoop? He wasn't only killing and using endangered animals, but he was also celebrating it as if it was an achievement with other friends and poachers.* Ben thought, disgusted. However, he knew he couldn't sabotage this mission. Too many people would be present, including guards and security, since a lot of powerful and rich poachers would be there.

If Ben jumped into it, it would be a suicide mission. He sighed. He knew what would help. Infiltrating the party and taking out all the poachers in one go would be impossible. That was why he needed his old team back. He could not do this alone. Not if he didn't want to die. He also knew that rescuing Dana was important, so he wasn't going to give up. He had to save her, and if he had to grovel at Jill and Stan's feet, then he would. He had to.

Chapter 13: Abandoned

"So, will you be joining us for drinks tonight at the bar?" Shirley asked.

Jill looked up from her computer and sighed, "I don't think I can, Shirley. Still have a lot of work to wrap up before I leave."

"It really is sad that you are never able to join us for drinks after work. It's become such a tradition with all of us," Shirley said, sounding a bit too haughty for Jill's tastes.

"Sorry," Jill said half-heartedly.

It was true that Jill was trying her best to adjust to her new workplace and coworkers. She had tried her hardest to make friends or at least jell with the rest of them. However, she couldn't help but feel left out. They had a lot of these "traditions" that Shirley spoke of. Apparently, the rest of them knew each other for years at this job while Jill was a new hire. It made her feel like she stood out for it, and Jill didn't like that feeling. It made her miss her previous job and coworkers. At the clinic, it used to feel like a family. Jacob, Sandra, Tony, and Ben. They were all like family to her, but here, she felt like an outsider.

It had been two weeks since Jill had joined this small company as an IT technician, but still, she felt a lot like she did when she was the new girl in high school. As a military brat, Jill had happened to move around a lot in her younger years. They would move around so many towns and cities that she stopped keeping track. It all became a blur, and faces started merging into one another. She remembered seeking therapy to understand why she didn't have any long-lasting friendships or relationships from that time period. She had harbored a lot of negativity for her father during that time.

This one time, she had to break up with her boyfriend of three months because they had to move so suddenly. After throwing her tantrum and telling her father how he was 'ruining her life,' Jill realized that people and things in life come and go. Nothing was permanent, and she couldn't hold on to people like they would be there forever. She realized at such a young age that everything was temporary and nobody would be in her life for a long time. So, she learned not to get so attached.

Meeting Ben and working for him was a transformation for Jill. She had joined the clinic because not only was it a small office and not anything too intense but also because Jill could see how sweet and kind Ben was. She had never met a man like him before and was also mature enough to admit that she even had a crush on him in the beginning. It fizzled out, though, and she felt like he was more family than anything. When she became so attached to the vet, she had no idea, but soon, she was apparently even willing to die for him.

Leaving her job at the clinic had been one of the hardest things Jill had had to do in the longest time. She didn't even know how much she had grown to love the place and the people until she had to leave it all behind. She remembered her conversation with Jacob about leaving very clearly.

"You're leaving?!" Jacob's sudden appearance in the break room made Jill pause in the middle of taking a bite. "And since when do you eat here?" Jacob's confusion with her antics was totally justified.

Jill had never eaten in the break room since her first day at that job. She had refused to, stating, "It feels lonely to be back there as if I am not important enough to join you guys for lunch." Since then, she had started eating with Ben or sometimes Jacob if Ben was unavailable.

Ben had always made her feel welcome since she joined, and she knew that was a rare quality in her boss that she would miss dearly when she looked for work elsewhere.

"Yes, I am leaving," Jill responded without any preamble.

Jacob stared at her for a few minutes, boring his eyes into her head as if he could pull out the answers from her brain just from the sheer force of his staring.

"Did something happen? You know you can talk to me, right? About anything." Jacob said in a soft whisper.

"I know. And nothing happened. I just needed a change. It's time to move on to bigger and better things," Jill replied diplomatically.

"That's bullshit, and you know it," Jacob didn't beat around the bush. "Did something happen with the doc? He seems quite upset, too."

Jill sighed and packed away the rest of her garden salad, "Nothing happened, Jake. I told you. I'm fine. And Ben is fine, too."

Jacob continued to try to talk to her after that, but Jill refused to share what had happened. Just because she was leaving and was not on talking terms with Ben didn't mean that she would ruin his plans or mission. She still believed in his cause, no matter what anyone else thought. She still hoped he would be successful and find a way to destroy Peter and his business, but she no longer wanted to be associated with it.

After their conversation that day, Jacob acted like he was mad at her for leaving. Deep down inside, Jill knew that he was just hurt that she would leave so suddenly and without any explanation. If she were in his place, she would be concerned, too. She was used to people coming and going in her life, but others weren't as much. Even so, she knew that leaving was the best option for her at the moment after everything that had happened. It was still too overwhelming for her, and she was still having nightmares about it weeks later.

It's not that Jill was a boring person or a scaredy-cat. She had been quite the wild child while growing up. Having to move so many times and barely retaining any long-term friends, Jill had learned to act out. She had gotten into video games from a very early age. She wasn't only into video games, but she was also into the violence and aggression of it. She knew she couldn't go out and be violent because her dad would literally ground her for life, but she had found an outlet.

She became a pro-gamer at only 16, and when she started competing with real adult men who had a lot of anger issues, Jill learned how bad it could actually get. Her education was suffering because of her not wanting to do anything but play video games all day, every day. Her parents would tell her to go out, meet new people, and make friends, but she didn't listen to them. They didn't know how hard it would be for her to leave them all after they had to move again.

Jill got into hacking, and that's when things became bad. She would hack into anyone's game and profile, not thinking much of it. Once she realized how good she really was, she started looking for more things to hack into. One day, she ended up hacking into the military database of the base they were staying at. Safe to say, her father almost lost his job and got court-martialed, and she got into a lot of trouble. That was not the end of it, though, because soon enough, there were people who were looking for her—people who had learned of her skills of being able to hack into military systems and those who were pissed at her for hacking into their own.

Those people turned out to be violent, bad people. That was when Jill realized the dangers of messing with things that were not her business. She knew then that she would never put her nose where it didn't belong and stay away from anything remotely violent. It wasn't a lesson that she learned the easy way either. It all happened very fast and very violently for her.

When Jill was 17, she was going through a lot in life. Her dad was still facing trouble and punishment from the government for how she had hacked into the military server. Her home life had never been too peaceful since they moved around a lot, and her parents' marriage was suffering too. Yet, it had never been too bad, not before then, at least. Jill had realized early on that she was the reason why her family suffered so greatly during that time. She had brought those struggles down upon everyone, and she would always carry that guilt with her.

Her parents had stopped talking to her because she refused to listen to them. They didn't know what to say to make her listen and understand that her path was too dangerous for her. Her dad had even tried to sit down and talk with her about it, but it didn't impact her as he thought it would.

"Jill," her dad said, sitting across from her. "You know how much trouble you've put me in, right?"

Jill looked down, "I have told you. I'm sorry about that."

"I know, honey," her dad sighed. "It's just that ... your mother and I are very concerned."

"I have told you I won't hack anymore," Jill said.

"I know, but you also refuse to give it up altogether," he said.

"So, what? You want me to give up on something I love? Something I am truly good at? Other parents usually encourage things like this, you know," Jill rebuked.

"They would never encourage their child wasting time on video games all day. No one will," her dad seemed upset. "You have to stop this. You have to focus on your studies and find something better to do with your life. You can't keep playing video games forever."

"Why not?!" Jill stood up, getting angry.

"Because it's not a career!" Her dad also yelled.

"I don't care!" Jill screamed and ran to her room.

After that day, she went back on her promise of no more hacking and continued to play video games. That was how she found herself on the dark web. She was too upset and angry about her parents not taking her or her passion seriously. She stopped caring what they thought and decided to do whatever she wanted. She thought they would never be able to find out anyways. She was wrong.

One day, when she was on the dark web, she received a message on a forum she frequented. The person was untraceable, of course, and was asking her about her hacking skills and how good she was. Then they pointed out how she had hacked into the U.S. military server, something that rang a warning bell inside her head. How did this person know? They told her that they were very impressed with her skills and wanted her to join their team of hackers.

Jill was told that they were a group of elite hackers who worked remotely and secretly for different purposes. At first, they presented themselves to her as internet vigilantes who were fighting evil corporations and corruption using their hacking skills. It was something that interested Jill very much. In her innocence, she thought that if she did something good like that, then maybe her parents would recognize her talent and understand that she was not doing anything wrong. Safe to say, that did not go the way her seventeen-year-old self was expecting. Jill got herself into the group, and soon enough, she became very close to the members. She didn't know their names, where they lived, how old they were, or even their gender identities. All she knew was that they shared a love for computers and video games. They would even play games together online, and Jill thought she had finally found her people. She felt like she belonged to this group of people.

It worked out perfectly for her because she didn't have to say goodbye to her new friends when it came time for them to move again. She could take them with her wherever she went. She was extremely happy about that, thinking that for once in her life, she could sustain friendships for a longer time and maybe even permanently. The group welcomed her with warmth and acceptance. They didn't judge her, mistreat her, or make her feel like she was unwelcome. Those were the feelings she felt at home with her family.

However, it all came crashing down one day in a horrible tragedy. The new town they had moved to was in Colorado. It was a quiet, sleepy, little town, and Jill had no intentions of putting down roots there. She would go to school just to appease her parents, not for actual academic gain. She was much smarter than her peers anyways. Even though she didn't want to create a long-lasting connection with the town, knowing they would move again eventually, she could not stop herself from developing a crush for a fellow senior.

He was cute, friendly, and very nice. He would help her with missed assignments because she would often flake out on classes for a session with her online friends. Brad was always there to help her. He understood her, accepted her for her weird and quirky traits, and liked her anyways. When they started dating, Jill was very happy. He was her first boyfriend, and she was absolutely smitten. Her parents were very happy too and thought that it meant Jill was finally letting go of her old habits. They were wrong, of course.

As her relationship with Brad started taking more and more of her attention, Jill stopped spending as much time with her hacker group of friends as much as she used to. She was happy going out with her boyfriend. Her parents were happy with her, and life was going pretty well for her after so long. She finally felt like her life was clicking into place until her online friends started demanding more of her.

The projects they participated in were illegal but never too bad. At least, their intentions were always good. To take down a corrupt politician, bankrupt a greedy corporation that refused to pay equal minimum wage, etc. Then one day, the group decided to rob a bank. The bank was known to have high interest rates and had caused many families to lose their homes to mortgages. They wanted to take down the bank, but they wanted to do it by robbing it and keeping all the money for themselves. It didn't sit right with Jill. She proposed that they give the money back to the families that had been affected, but they didn't listen to her. That was the first time they showed her any negativity, and it was so intense that it scared her. Then when she refused to help them with the project, they started becoming scarier and more intense. It escalated to threats that, at first, Jill brushed off. Then when they started threatening her family, friends, and especially Brad, she knew she was in over her head. She had to do something — tell someone. So, she went to her dad and told him everything. At first, he was mad at her, really mad at her, but then he agreed to help her. They decided to go to the authorities because that was the safest bet. The one thing she didn't do was not tell Brad because she didn't want him to get scared and break up with her.

As tragedies go, hindsight is twenty-twenty. Once they went to the authorities, the hackers grew even more upset. They became aggressive, because they had been exposed by one of their own, and their threats became even more terrifying. Then one day, it all came to a brutal end. She had gone to see Brad at his house, hoping to talk to him and tell him everything. However, when she reached his house, she saw red and blue flashing lights everywhere. She rushed ahead and saw police cars, paramedics, neighbors, and Brad's parents all in chaos. Then the paramedics were wheeling a body out. Brad's mother was beside herself in tears as his father held her and tried not to break at the sight of their young son's dead body.

That was the day Jill decided she was done with it all. She was done with hacking; she was done with everything. She always blamed herself for Brad's death, because she knew the truth even though the media was told he died in a freak home invasion accident. She knew that she had messed with the wrong people and got the worst punishment in turn. It took Jill a long time to cope with Brad's death. She was clinically depressed, and her parents sent her to a medical care facility. Once she had gotten better, she came out wanting to make Brad's death just and fair.

That was the day she decided that she was going to use her skills only for the good of the people. She would make sure bad people got to pay, but she would remain as far from bad company as possible. That was why she chose to switch from her high-paying job at a multinational company to Ben's veterinary clinic.

Jill wanted to enhance her skills, so she went to college to become the tech expert that she was. That was why when she agreed to go with Ben, she was hesitant. She only did it because she realized that she could not let Ben go alone and because he would most probably end up getting killed. If Jill knew she could do something to prevent that, she would. She had agreed to help Ben because she couldn't have another death on her conscience. Never again. Not if she could help it.

Nevertheless, Jill didn't know it could get so dangerous and violent. She still heard the gunshots in her dreams and felt as if Peter's men were still chasing her. Although she had moved on from her previous job and Ben, she couldn't let go of the past entirely. Jill didn't know why, but this time it was taking her longer than usual to get over friendships and people, maybe because she had actually allowed herself to get attached for the first time in so long. The next day, as the morning light hit Jill's closed eyelids, she woke up with a groan. Then she realized she had slept through her alarm and rushed out of bed to get ready for work. She immediately sent a text to Shirley, telling her how sorry she was for being late. Shirley, on the other hand, just told her to take it easy since they were all suffering too. Apparently, going drinking on a weekday was not going well for any of them. Jill pretended to be shocked.

After taking a shower, getting dressed in a navy-blue jumpsuit, and pairing it up with a denim jacket, Jill let her natural curls flow wild and free. She didn't have time to put on much makeup, so she just grabbed cereal and munched away. Her hot cup of coffee almost burned her throat and tongue, but she braved through it. Then she left a text for her mom, asking what her plans were for the day.

Jill's daily routine was like that. She would almost always wake up in a rush, either from the effects of her nightmares or because she was still used to waking up early for her clinic job. Since this job allowed her more time to sleep, she wasn't used to the new time changes.

She would always eat a bowl of cereal, feeling guilty every time because she had promised her mother that she would take care of herself and eat a proper breakfast every day. Jill and her mother spoke almost every day, and every day her mother would make her promise.

Her mother would say, "Eat well and not exist on cereals alone! Do you hear me?"

Jill loved her mother, but she also loved cereal. Sue her for liking the breakfast of the champions. It was the one good thing about waking up. Not being a morning person was probably one of the most non-Jill things for her to be, yet that's how she was. Her energy and excitement for the day didn't start until she actually left for work. What most didn't realize was that the reason she was always so peppy and energetic was that she genuinely loved her work. Every day was a new challenge, even if it was some employee forgetting their password fifth time in a row. She loved computers, and the work brought her satisfaction. It was mostly her need to be in control, and with her job, she got to be in so much control.

That need for control was also what drove her to join Ben's crazy mission. She thought that if she were to take care of things, then perhaps it wouldn't get so bad. She thought that if she kept everything in control, they could get in and out without any dangerous events occurring or any need for violence. However, now she realized that she should've known better. Jill should have known that bringing people like Stan and his group would definitely result in violence.

At first, she had been hesitant to work with Dana and the rest of the people. She didn't know them, so she could not trust them. She didn't know what their intentions were or why they wanted to be joined with Ben's mission. It didn't make sense to Jill. Dana and Stan were powerful enough on their own to bring him down. So, why did they need Ben to join them so badly? As she munched away on her cereal, she thought about how she was so unsure at first. Then Ben talked to her and calmed her down.

"Jill, I know why you're so hesitant to trust them. I get it. But, you trust me, right?"

That was what Ben had said. She had trusted Ben, and that led her to the lion's den. Literally. Jill still felt hurt and betrayed, but she knew she couldn't hold on to such feelings for too long. She might have been influenced by Ben's words and actions, but she had made the decision to go along with the mission herself. She knew she couldn't blame Ben for her actions; it wasn't fair. For what it was worth, she knew that Ben hadn't planned to get them all in mortal danger either.

Ben was a good man and only had the best intentions. His entire mission was to save exotic wild animals around the world, for crying out loud. How good can a man get? Jill knew that she was mostly upset because she had been wrong about her own ideas and had not been in control of things. That was what pissed her off so much. Sure, being fired at was also not fun, but she didn't like how she had lost control of the situation so quickly. It had almost cost them their lives, and for that, she felt guilty. That was something she never told Ben because she didn't want him to feel bad.

Jill knew that Ben would have tried to make her feel better, but it wouldn't have worked. She knew that if she had been more in control and had handled things better, then things wouldn't have turned so drastically dangerous. Thinking about it all again made her miss the gang, though. As Jill got done with her breakfast and washed the dishes, she realized how they had all bonded over the course of one small mission. They had gotten along surprisingly well.

If somebody had told Jill that she would get along with such people just a few days ago, she would have laughed in their face. She thought Dana was a stuck-up, Stan was hungry for violence, and his men were just too dumb to find their own thing to do.

Jill knew that she was unfair with her presumptions, but she didn't want to like them. However, over their mission, they had each other's backs. She had never had people help her stay alive with such intensity before.

During that night, while they were so focused on catching Peter and saving that tiger, Jill had seen the way they had all come to work together. It was surprising, but she was glad to have joined them. She knew she couldn't have had better people to watch her back. Thinking about them all again made her miss them in an unexpected turn of events. Before she could go further down the memory lane or miss the people she had known for such a short time, her cell phone rang.

She wiped her hands on a dishrag and swiped the screen to answer without even looking, thinking it was probably just Shirley asking where she was.

"Hey, Shirley. Don't worry, I'm on my way-," Jill started but was interrupted by a voice she hadn't been expecting.

"Jill," Ben's gruff voice spoke on the other line, and Jill was silenced.

"Ben?" Jill asked in a whisper, not expecting him, of all people, to call her so early.

"Hey, how are you?" Ben said in a weary voice.

Jill could tell that there was something wrong almost immediately. She had spent enough time with the man to know when there was something amiss by just listening to his voice. "Is everything okay? You sound ... weird."

"Yeah," he chuckled without any real amusement in his voice. "I kind of need you."

"What is it? What's wrong?" Jill was on alert. It didn't matter if she was supposed to be mad at him or if she didn't have time to listen to him. Ben needed her, and that was all she focused on.

"Um, I sort of called Dana, but it didn't go as expected. I called her, but Peter picked up instead," Ben explained.

"What?!" Jill gasped.

"Yeah, and he didn't tell me where she was or anything else. He just taunted me and then hung up. I had to track him down, but I still cannot find him. I need your help, Jill. I need my best IT girl," Ben said with a huffed laugh.

"Of course. Where are you?" Jill already had her laptop out and opened it on the kitchen counter.

Ben explained to her how he had gone to the jungle, tracked Rahul, and then gone to the compound, only to find it abandoned. Jill was not shocked to hear that since she knew Peter would have vacated that area pretty soon after it was discovered by Ben and Stan. Then Ben told her how he had found out about his other headquarters in the city, and Jill couldn't help but chuckle.

"Wow, you did that all on your own, huh?" Jill said wryly as she tapped away on her keyboard. She already had a lock on Ben's location.

"Yeah," Ben chuckled, too. "Now I know I have no right to call you out of the blue like this and ask for your help, especially since I said I would give you the space you needed to come to terms with everything. But, I really need your help, Jill. I can't do this on my own. I can't find him or take him down on my own. I have tried for years, but look where that got me. And only a few days with you guys could get me close enough to kill Peter."

Jill could hear the desperation clearly in Ben's voice. She could tell how the situation must have been too much to handle and how much it must have taken for him to go against his word and call Jill like this.

"I cannot let Dana get hurt, Jill. I need to help her. Save her. Please, tell me you will help me," Ben pleaded.

It hurt Jill to see Ben so unsure and desperate for help. She felt guilty for making him think as if she would not help him in such circumstances.

"Of course, I will help, Ben. Don't worry about it. I would never leave you in a lurch like this, no matter what happens between us. And we would get Dana back, don't worry. I'm coming," Jill promised him.

After calling Shirley and making up an excuse as to why she suddenly couldn't make it to work, she drove over to where Ben was. He had gone back to camping in the jungle, hoping Peter or any of his men would make an appearance again so he could interrogate them some more. She had never seen this side of Ben before, but she had always known that underneath his calm and collected exterior was an unleashed anger and aggression that would only come out for people like Peter.

As Ben and Jill met up, she could see the apology all over his face. He immediately started apologizing to her for bothering her like this, but she stopped him before he could get too far.

"Stop that. You know I consider you family, and families have each other's backs, okay? Stop apologizing and help me figure out where that bastard is," Jill said in a no-nonsense tone.

As Jill and Ben sat in his camp, keeping an eye for any visitors or people nearby, Jill kept trying to search for Peter.

"I can never thank you enough for this, Jill. Seriously," Ben said.

"Didn't I tell you to stop that?" Jill said without looking away from her computer as her fingers continued to fly over the keyboard.

Ben had never seen her work so hard on something before. He smiled, knowing that Jill was truly one of the best people he had ever met.

"Are you just gonna sit there or be useful?"

Ben chuckled and started gathering a few weapons to venture out again. He was going to do another perimeter check to make sure they hadn't missed any new appearances or people coming by. It could be Peter or his men, and Ben could not afford to lose that chance.

"Wait!" Jill suddenly shouted, then immediately remembered they were supposed to be quiet. "Sorry," she said sheepishly.

"Well, what is it?" Ben asked.

"I think I've got it," Jill said.

"What?" Ben was shocked. "You found him?!"

"Yep," Jill said proudly.

Chapter 14: One on One

After Jill got a location on Dana and Peter, Ben immediately went into action. He knew he had to capitalize on time because it had already been a day and a half since he had called on Dana's phone and Peter had picked up. He guessed that he must have taken her a day or two before then. Whatever the timeline of her kidnapping, Ben knew he had to find Dana fast. There was no time to waste, and he had to use everything he had and put in as much effort as he could.

"Okay, so what's the plan?" Jill asked, looking ready to go.

"Jill," Ben sighed. "I can't make you follow me. Not again. Not after what happened the last time. I only wanted your help with finding Peter's location, but now you can go home. Your work here is done."

The shock that passed through Jill's face was enough to make Ben silent.

"Are you dismissing me? Seriously?! After I helped you find this man? You are seriously telling me to go home?" Jill was flabbergasted.

Ben was stumped. "The last time I had you come with me, things didn't go so well. It almost ruined our friendship. I'm not even sure if it's still alright. Jill, I can't make you do something you don't want to do. Again. I know this kinda stuff is way past your limits, so I'm just going to go by myself."

"Wow," Jill looked hurt. "After everything we've been through together, it is so easy for you to just cut ties like that."

"I'm not cutting ties!" Ben said. "I just don't want you to go with me on another mission, get into more hostile situations, and end up hating me again."

"You think I hate you?" Now Jill was the one who was confused. "I could never hate you, Ben. You are one of my closest friends. Yes, I was upset about what happened on the mission, but this time I know what the risks are and what the mission entails. This time, I want to go with you. Even if it puts my life in danger, I can't let you go alone there! You'll be handicapped without me."

Ben had to say that she was right. He would be lost without her, but he wasn't ready to sacrifice their friendship for a mission again. "You sure you wanna do this?" He had to make sure.

"Yes," Jill said. "I wouldn't have recommended if I wasn't."

Ben thought about it for a few long minutes, weighing the pros and cons of the situation. He knew that having Jill by his side would be his best-case scenario. He could not expect to win just by himself. He needed her expertise and skills to take down Peter and rescue Dana. The situation had become so much more dangerous than the last time, because this time, Peter had one of the people who were important to Ben. He couldn't afford to make any mistake this time or have Peter find out he was coming beforehand.

The only one who could help Ben accomplish that and complete the mission with success was Jill. He knew he was lost without her. He didn't want their friendship to suffer, but if Jill was still suggesting to come along herself, he couldn't say no. *Saying no now might do even more damage*, Ben thought.

"Okay, then I guess you're coming with me," Ben sighed.

A huge smile spread across Jill's face, and she jumped up and down, clapping her hands like a seal. Ben almost laughed at the sight. He had missed his preppy, hyper best friend.

As they got down to discuss the details, Jill helped Ben tinker with a few things until their plan was perfect. They both knew what was at stake — Dana's life. So, they knew they couldn't go in blindly, guns blazing. They had to find a way to get in, rescue Dana, and get out. Once they had Dana with them, safe and sound, then Ben could go after Peter with no loose ends behind.

"One thing," Ben said.

Jill looked up from the computer screen where she was following Peter's footsteps. Literally, how she managed to do that was out of Ben's comprehensive skills. This was exactly why he had called Jill, though. She could do things that Ben couldn't even think of.

"What's up?" Jill asked.

"I forgot to tell you something," Ben responded. "When I interrogated one of Peter's men for his location, he told me something. He said there was going to be a party of some sort. Peter arranged a get-together for his poaching friends, and they're all going to come together to have a huge poaching celebration."

"What the...?" Jill was disgusted.

"I know," Ben shook his head, trying to dispel the disgust himself. He could never understand how people could be so sick.

"So, I'm guessing all the big names in the poaching business are to be there?" Jill inquired, already clicking on her keyboard, trying to find out more.

"Yeah, I figured," Ben said.

"Okay, yeah, you're right. The information checks out," Jill said while looking at her laptop.

"It does?" Ben came closer to take a look himself.

"Yeah, there have been orders placed by Peter's secretary for catering, decoration, even a DJ of all things," Jill made a face at that. "But, yeah, they're definitely having a party."

Ben groaned and said, "So, can you see who has been invited?"

Jill scoffed, "Please. Of course, I can."

Ben smirked and watched her work her magic on the computer. Soon, she had somehow found the guest list and started researching the names off it.

"Okay, so, our first guest is Jacob Reeds. He is in his fifties, runs a multimillionaire poaching ring, and has close ties with the Russian mafia. Nice," Jill remarked sarcastically.

Then she moved on, "We have Scott Cornick, some Scottish poacher who's coming in on Peter's request. There's David Byers, another American poacher. There's Vishay Kumar, some poaching 'prince' from India. There're Maestro and Alex Pierce, twins from Italy. A Jennifer Kim coming in from Seoul with her gangster husband. Oh, and there's a billionaire flying in from Dubai, someone named Edward Coles. They're all coming with their entire posse."

Ben just listened to the names, trying to retain them in his head, because he knew he would need to remember them later on. They were all Peter, just with different names. They were all monsters who only cared about money and nothing else.

"So, these are the top names in the business as well. They have built empires upon empires off their poaching business. Some are even bigger than the mafia in their own country. Some are backed by the mafia. This is all so convoluted and disgusting, ugh," Jill kept informing Ben while he listened silently.

"Seriously, Ben. These men are dangerous, arrogant, and filthy rich. They have people in the government, the police force, everywhere ... are you up for this?"

Ben just looked at her, "You think I'm not?"

"I just don't want you to go in blindly. These are some of the most dangerous men coming together in one place. These men know how to fight and get rid of roadblocks, Ben. You are a roadblock now, too. If they hurt you, you won't be able to hit back. They have a lot of power, and I just don't want you to take on something that's so much bigger than you," Jill said, concerned.

"Jill, I know what you're saying, and I know that you're right. But I have been waiting for this for years. I have to do this. Even if I don't end up making much of a difference, I would know that I tried. That's all I need to do. And if I have you by my side, I know I can achieve the impossible," Ben said assuredly.

Jill looked at the vet closely, trying to see any signs of fear, doubt, or insecurity. There was none. She knew that Ben was dedicated to his cause more than he was dedicated to anything else in his life.

"Well, if you're so adamant about it, I guess I can help you out. Try to keep you from getting killed at least," Jill rolled her eyes jokingly. She knew the risks that lay ahead and was trying to keep herself distracted from that. If she didn't, she might just break down.

"Okay, then, let's get this show on the road!" Ben exclaimed.

It was time to rescue Dana and meet Peter once again.

***

"I have eyes on the prize," Jill spoke into Ben's ear through the communications device.

"What? You have found Dana?" Ben mumbled quietly, trying his hardest not to draw any attention to himself.

"Oh, is that the code for Dana? My bad. I meant the poachers. The gangsters. What did we decide for them? Eagle?" Jill ranted on confusedly.

"Never mind," Ben sighed.

"Okay, well, I have eyes on the guests as they arrive," Jill informed him.

"Right, well, keep your eyes peeled for anything sus...," Ben got interrupted by Jill exclaiming.

"Ooh, boy! They have not spared any expenses, have they? Look at those ball gowns and diamonds! I also see some hidden weapons. Ben, if I wasn't sure, I'd think I was watching an episode from *The Crown* or *Gossip Girl*. How rich are these people? I thought it was going to be just a little beer pong, some cheap liquor, maybe some disco lights ... I wasn't expecting a ball!" Jill rambled on.

"Jill? Can we stay focused, please?" Ben said.

"Oh, right. Sorry," Jill said sheepishly.

Ben and Jill were currently monitoring the party that Peter was hosting. At first, they had come across a puzzle as to how Ben could enter the premises without being noticed. Peter knew him now, and they were sure that every guard and the hired lackey were going to know who Ben was. They couldn't just walk in. Ben had suggested disguising themselves as party guests, but Jill pointed out that it could have backfired because what if somebody recognized that they weren't who they said they were. These poachers could know each other by face. She had also mentioned that maybe someone would recognize Ben, too.

Then they came up with the idea that Ben would go in as a hotel guest, not a party guest. Anyone was allowed to go to the hotel; they were sure Peter wouldn't waste his resources on such a big night to watch every guest who checked into the hotel. He would mostly be making sure that the guests for the party were checked, and that's it. Jill had arranged a booking for him already, so it didn't seem suspicious that he was a walk-in patron on the night of the party.

Ben was dressed in normal clothes; a baggy hoodie, a flannel, a trucker's hat, and some spectacles. The less he looked like himself, the better the chances were that nobody would recognize him. Jill decided to stay hidden, opting to work from the van so she could monitor and keep an eye on everything that happened inside.

She wasn't going to make the same mistake as the last time. This time, they were in a public place, so Jill could keep a close eye on everything that went on. Ben was currently sitting in the lobby, pretending to work on his laptop, while he waited for Jill to inform him of everything going on inside the party that was taking place inside the hotel's ballroom.

As for Dana, they still hadn't been able to find her exact location. They knew that she was in Peter's captivity, but where he was keeping her was still a mystery.

"Still no signs of Dana?" Ben asked.

"No," Jill sighed. She was looking for any signs that could point toward where she was being held, but nothing showed up.

As time passed, more and more guests arrived.

"Ben...," Jill said.

"What?" He asked.

"These guys are loaded. And I don't mean money or fries. I mean weapons. So far, I have counted double the amount of people showing up. They're all carrying specialized, customized, or black-market guns that aren't even permitted in the USA. Some of these weapons are so rare that you cannot be a good person in order to get them. I saw a Weatherby Orion, 12 gauge; a Remington 7400; a Smith and Wesson target pistol...," Jill said.

"Don't worry, Jill. They are gangsters of sorts. Of course, they would carry such weapons. We're just here to observe them, for now. Dana is our priority," Ben reassured her. He knew that seeing such weapons would make Jill nervous, especially since she was so against violence of any sort.

"Yeah," Jill sighed.

An hour passed by, and the guests had all arrived. Then came in the host of the hour, the man of the party — Peter.

"Oh, he's here," Jill announced, and Ben immediately knew who she was talking about.

Peter arrived with a flair, as was expected. He was wearing a customized Gucci suit, with his initials embroidered over the left breast pocket. His gold-toed shoes were the highlight and, of course, the huge rifle that he was carrying. He was carrying a Winchester Model, 16 gauge, in his hands, showing it off proudly to his criminal friends. He looked chipper and excited, like the cat that ate the mouse.

"Someone seems happy," Jill's dry comment almost made Ben chuckle even though he was too busy trying to tamper down the rage he felt boiling up in his veins as soon as he heard his name.

"Where's Dana? Any sign of her? If he's there, she must be nearby," Ben said.

"No, I still don't see her. That's so weird," Jill said, confused by what was happening.

Before coming to the hotel, they had figured that Dana was going to be with Peter because Peter knew that Ben was coming to the hotel, and he wouldn't want an asset like Dana to be compromised. Ben and Jill thought that he might even show up with Dana at his side, forcing her to be at a party of criminals that she couldn't expose or bring to justice. It would be sick but right up to Peter's alley. Although, now that Peter was at the party, drinking and laughing his way around with the guests, Ben and Jill were both confused. If Dana wasn't with him, then where was she? Why did he look so calm and happy?

As their minds ran wild with theories and they tried to figure out what was going on, Peter started greeting the guests with a speech of his.

"Ugh, now he's giving a speech," Jill commented.

"Forget him. Find Dana," Ben said with a rush.

"I'm trying, Ben, but there are literally no signs of her. I have no idea where she could be. I hate to think of it, but the only reason Peter could be so happy and not have Dana by his side is if...," Jill didn't finish her sentence.

Ben clenched his fists, closed his eyes, and clenched his jaw as he tried to dispel those thoughts. He would kill Peter if he hurt a hair on Dana's head.

"Wait," Jill interrupted Ben's murderous thoughts.

"What?" Ben asked.

"Ben, you know that Peter is not stupid, right? He wouldn't make a stupid mistake as to leave Dana in some unknown basement and go party uptown while he knows that you're on his tail. Right?" Jill said.

"Yeah, so?" He was lost.

"He would make sure that his best bargaining chip with you, Dana, is safe and sound. Near him. Right?" Jill continued.

"What are you getting at?" Ben didn't have time for games.

"I'm saying that even Peter knows not to leave Dana until he is within a few meters from her. At this point, she's the only thing keeping him safe from you. Otherwise, you could just walk in there right now and shoot him. The end," Jill explained.

"Believe me, I have the urge," Ben said dryly.

"Ben, listen to me. Peter would not let Dana be too far from him. Not tonight. Not when he knows you're coming after him. He would keep her close just to use her against you. Like he did with the tiger. So, what I am saying is that Dana has to be close.

Really close. Peter looks too calm and peaceful to have left her somewhere far away," Jill said.

Ben's mind ran in double the speed. Jill was right. Peter wouldn't make a stupid mistake like that. He knew how important Dana was. Not just to Ben, but generally. She was a public figure. He wouldn't let her leave his side or be too far away.

"If she's not in his sight, she's still close by," Jill deduced.

"She's in the hotel," Ben finished.

Jill immediately started tapping away on her keyboard, trying to get an eye on every room in the place. She hacked into the records to see which rooms Peter had booked for the night. Dana had to be in one of those rooms.

Ben got up and went inside the elevator, asking Jill, "Which floor?"

"He has booked three suites. They're all on the 27th floor. 272, 273, and 274. Go!" Jill hurried Ben.

Ben cursed the slow speed of the elevator, never feeling more rushed in his life than he did at that moment.

"Ben, listen, I know you want to go in guns blazing, but you have to be smart about this. Peter must have his best men posted outside and inside the room she's in. Don't do anything heroic or stupid," Jill said just as Ben reached the floor and got out of the elevator.

He spotted the hired man outside 272, immediately going up to him and clocking him on the head before he could even punch Ben.

"Too late," Ben grunted as he punched the man in his stomach.

The man groaned and went down to his knees immediately. Even though the man was huge and burly, he was no match for Ben's Krav Maga.

"Ben!" Jill yelled.

The guy stood back up with a groan and came at Ben with fury in his eyes. He was pale, with a bald head and tattoos on his face.

"Ben, I can see you! Stop! He has a gun! He can shoot!" Jill screamed in his ears.

Ben punched the guy as he came at him, but the guy punched him right back. Ben went to give him a flying kick in the stomach then, and the man went sprawling back on the floor. Ben got on top of him and started punching him straight in the face repeatedly. The man wasn't giving up, though, and reached up to strangle Ben's throat. His meaty hands wrapped around Ben's throat and squeezed. Ben could feel his windpipe almost being crushed as he coughed and wheezed. Ben stopped punching him and tried to go limp to fool him into thinking Ben was surrendering. Just as he did so, the guy's grip on his throat loosened a bit, and Ben took the opportunity to reach out and punch the man in his throat with all his might. His windpipe was definitely crushed. Ben got out of his grip and stood up as the man clutched his throat and wheezed. Ben could feel his eyes water as he stood up, trying to get air back into his lungs as his throat throbbed with excruciating pain.

The other guy groaned in pain but then stood back up. Ben groaned, too, not liking the fact that he had to keep fighting the huge guy.

"Jesus! He's not going down!" Jill yelled in his ear.

The man then pulled out a gun, and Jill could be heard screaming in Ben's ears to run or hide. "Do something, you idiot doctor!" she said when the door behind him opened, and this guy was suddenly hit on the back of his head with a lamp. Ben stared in shock as the huge guy, probably over 200 pounds, went down like a sack of potatoes. Just as his body fell to the floor, Ben looked up and saw the person who hit him. Dana.

***

The sudden sounds of fighting outside the door had alerted Dana to something strange happening outside the suite. The three men inside the room also became alert and looked at the door. Dana knew that the Russian guy posted outside was built like a building, so they wouldn't last if someone was trying to fight him. Dana was still hopeful, though. It meant that someone had come to rescue her. Not that she needed rescuing, she was doing fine on her own. Yes, she was a little worse for the wear, but it was all going well. She had it under control. When Peter had kidnapped her the night she was coming home from work, she had been shocked and afraid. She knew that she had no way of alerting anyone, and even if her disappearance made some splash in the news, nobody would be able to find her, because she was back at Peter's compound. She couldn't even tell Ben. However, her cloud of desperation and fear had dissipated almost instantly when Peter started talking.

Either he was really stupid, or he underestimated Dana and thought she was really stupid. The moment he started talking to her, he started spilling all the beans. The one thing that upset her was that she had no way of recording it, but she was still getting tons of information from the man himself. Dana had a photographic memory, something Peter obviously didn't know. He probably counted on the fact that since Dana couldn't record him, anything he said was okay because she couldn't prove it later on.

Peter really underestimated her.

Dana's memory would help her remember everything Peter said to her while in captivity, and then when she went back home because she would, she would be able to research and investigate those things. What Peter had not been banking on was that Dana was one of the country's best journalists. She could investigate and put Peter away for almost all the things he confessed to in her presence.

So, ever since then, Dana had been playing the part of the poor kidnapped girl who was hysterical and desperate to go home. Dana was just biding time. She was gathering information from Peter while she plotted out her escape. She knew she just needed to get away from the compound, and then she could escape easily. She wasn't scared of his men or Peter himself. It just sucked that her role also meant that she had to suffer through torture and injuries.

Of course, she wasn't alright, but she was handling it very well. Then when Peter told her about the party, she knew that it was her time to escape. She just had to wait for the perfect opportunity. It seemed like the perfect opportunity had just presented itself.

"Can I get some water?" she croaked out, pretending to have a parched throat.

The blond-haired man was the one with the worst temper. He looked at her once and got up to get her some water. As he brought the glass close to her face, she drank some and then held it in her mouth. Just as he put the glass away, she sprayed the water in his face, startling him for a second. That second was just enough for Dana to jump along with the chair she was tied to and come down on his foot hard with one of the chair's legs. He screamed and cursed while the other two got near to hold her back. She swiveled her chair and broke the glass that was on the table. Then she hit the other two with the legs of the chair, swinging it with her body to hurt them as much as she could. Her upper body strength was one of her best qualities. Then while the other two went down, groaning in pain as one clutched his leg and the other clutched his stomach, the mean one stood up to grab her. She quickly pushed him away with the chair and then bent down to pick up a big glass shard with her mouth. While she was on the ground, two of them came and held her there by her nape.

"You little conniving bi...," before the mean, blond one could finish cursing at her, she quickly pushed her head back and hit him in the nose. It immediately started bleeding.

"Shit! You broke my nose!" he screamed in pain.

The other two came to grab her, but she started moving on the ground with the chair at her back so hard that they couldn't get a grip on her. Then one of them tried to put a hand on her mouth, and she used the glass shard she was holding with her teeth to cut his palm open. He immediately pulled back, and Dana took the chance to turn on her side so quickly that she hit the other guy with the back of the chair. Then she rolled on top of him with the chair on his chest as she faced the ceiling. She put all her force into her body to make the chair bounce on his body so it would hurt as much as possible.

The man screamed underneath her, trying his hardest to get her off, but the chair blocked his arms. The man came at her with a roar, but she quickly rolled back to the other side, and the man fell on top of the one that was writhing in pain on the floor.

Then the third one came and picked up her chair, hitting her in the face. She just smirked at him and then smacked her head to his forehead. She was disoriented and dizzy for a second as the hit made her head throb like her skull had been broken. As the man went down, she quickly bent forward to cut the ties on her wrists, binding her hands to the arms of the chair. As her hands got free, she held the glass shard in her palm. The mean one came at her again from behind and hit her over the head, but she ducked just in time. Then she quickly cut the ties around her ankles and stood up by throwing the chair back, so it hit the two behind her in the face. Then, without giving them time to get back up again, she went and stabbed them both in the neck with the glass shard.

She saw the third one get up in her periphery, holding his head and swaying a bit. She ran at him and stabbed him in both the knees so he could not walk. As the three went down, she threw the glass piece away and walked toward the door. There was a little mirror right near the door, and she noticed the blond, mean one coming at her from behind, neck bleeding profusely.

Dana quickly reached out, grabbed the lamp on the table right beside the door, and turned to hit him right over the head. He went down in a second. Then she opened the door and saw that the Russian man was about to shoot Ben, much to her shock. She quickly reached out and hit him over the head with the lamp she still held in her hand. Ben could only stare at her in utter shock.

"Dana?!" Ben exclaimed.

"Hi, Ben," Dana greeted him with a friendly smile, panting as if she hadn't just hit a huge guy and made him unconscious.

"What the hell...," Ben mumbled.

Dana was wearing a black jumpsuit that was more than a little wrinkled. Clearly, she hadn't gotten the chance to change after she got kidnapped. Her hair was a mess and all over the place, her makeup was smudged, and the mascara tracks on her face were dry and obviously days old. She had a busted lip, a bruise on her cheek, and her left foot seemed to be hurt too. She was barefoot as well. Ben finally got up off the floor and peeked inside the room she had just gotten out of. From his point of view, Ben could see three men sprawled out on the floor of the suite.

"Did you fight them on your own?" Ben asked in shock.

"What? I know Krav Maga," Dana shrugged.

"And you chose now to use it?" Ben asked, still in shock.

"I chose the right time to use it. The time when I could escape," Dana explained.

Suddenly, the stairwell door opened at the end of the hallway, and Ben was shocked to see Jill running up to them.

"Jill?" Ben and Dana asked simultaneously.

"We have to hurry. More of them are coming. They spotted the van, and I have to leave," Jill said in a rush. Then she stopped to take a look around, inside the room Dana had escaped from and the men lying everywhere. "What the hell happened here?"

"She knows Krav Maga," Ben shrugged as a way of explanation.

Jill just stared at Dana in awe, then she snapped out of it and wrapped her arms around the girl tightly, "Dana! Oh my god! Are you okay? I was so worried! We were both worried! Ben was freaking out! When he called me, I had to help! I can't believe they did that to you! I'll shoot him myself for you!"

Before Jill could ramble on any further and choke the life out of Dana, Ben gently pulled Jill away from her. "Aren't we supposed to be running?"

"Oh, right!" Jill exclaimed, then said, "This way!"

She ran ahead as Ben and Dana just looked at each other. They all got into the elevator, and Jill pushed the button for the third floor. Ben didn't ask any questions, just let her lead.

"So, how did this happen? How did he catch you?" Jill asked Dana.

"Well, I wasn't going to sit around and wait for something to happen. I went looking on my own. I happened to follow him on one of his hunting trips, and he saw me. He took me back to the compound, then he shifted me somewhere else. It's all such a blur. Tonight, I woke up in the hotel room and heard his men talking about the party. I knew it was my chance to escape. I'm just glad you guys are here," Dana said.

It was apparent that she was shaken up by the entire ordeal. Though, Ben and Jill were both glad to have her back in one piece. As the doors of the elevator opened, the three were about to walk out, but then they were faced with a bunch of guns being pointed in their faces.

Chapter 15: The Aftermath

"Hello, there, Ben!" Peter announced loudly as he stood in the center with several of his henchmen around him, pointing their guns at the trio's faces. "Long time no see!"

Ben felt his anger take over him. He did not want to mess with anything before because Dana was still in Peter's custody, but now there was nothing holding him back. He thought back to the last time he had seen Peter's evil face in person. He had let him get away, thinking that he would get to him before anything bad could happen. However, that had been one of the worst decisions of Ben's life. Saving the tiger was his priority, but he still could have shot Peter before driving away.

Because of that one moment of wrong decision-making, Ben had let his one chance slip away from him. That one chance could have changed and prevented so many things that followed. Because of that one wrong decision, Ben had lost his team. He hadn't only lost the new friends and comrades who he had found, but he also lost their faith in him.

Because of that one moment, he had lost his friendship with Jill. She had lost all trust in him, having no faith whatsoever in his capabilities to make sure that nothing would go wrong. They had lost the carefree and close friendship that they had cultivated over the time they had worked together.

Because of that one moment, Dana had gotten kidnapped. She had been taken against her will, and her life was put in danger, all because Ben didn't have the guts to pull the trigger.

He was too weak to let his hesitance in killing a living creature go and just shoot. If he had just shot Peter that day, none of it would have happened. They would've all been safe, and he wouldn't have lost everything he had.

Just the reminder of everything made Ben rage like never before. Before he could pounce on the man, Dana and Jill grabbed his arms tightly to stop him.

"Ben," Jill hissed in his ear. "Not now! Look at the number of guns they have!"

Ben took notice of the ten or twelve men who were gathered around Peter, all holding a rifle or gun of some kind in their hands. Ben didn't care much for his safety at the moment, but he would rather die than put the ladies in danger. He shook off the women's hands gently and tried to calm himself down. He had to wait for his turn, but he was sure it would come. He wasn't letting Peter get away this time. Not again.

"Now, before I have to use less than pleasing means to force you, why don't you guys come with us of your own volition, hmm? Come on; I'll give you a tour of my place. New place, actually," Peter laughed as if he had made the joke of the century.

He signaled slightly to his men, and they all grabbed Ben, Dana, and Jill by the arms, dragging them behind Peter's entourage. However, before they could be led to a truck or vehicle of some sort, Peter took them into the ballroom where the party was taking place.

"Ladies and gentlemen! I know I've made you antsy with my sudden exit, but now I am back!"

The audience waited to hear what Peter had to say, considering he had three people in his men's custody at the moment, at gunpoint to say the least.

"To explain myself, let me first introduce you to someone really special. Ben! Come forward, please, and greet our esteemed guests," Peter said.

The men shoved Ben forward, pointing a gun at the back of his head, and he was forced to take a few steps ahead until there was a spotlight shining down on him. He squinted under the bright light as Peter continued to talk.

"This here is Ben. One of my oldest *friends*. He is one of the most tenacious, if not the most determined, people I have ever met. This man has made it his life's mission to capture me!" Peter said dramatically.

The audience chuckled at that as if the idea of Peter being captured was so impossible.

"No matter our differences, I do like him a lot. The fact that he thinks he can take me down is ... endearing, to say the least."

The audience laughed yet again.

Ben felt his veins boiling with anger. This entire time, he was being presented to the crowd as if he was some precious prey that Peter had caught. Like one of the animals, he had poached. Ben felt sick at the thought.

His entire life, he had worked hard to find the man who had given him nightmares for life. He wanted to find Peter and make him pay for all the things he had done. He had tried his best to find him and make sure that his business suffered. Now that they were near the end of the road, Ben had also made some discoveries.

Peter was only one man of an entire organization. There were so many other people who had created a living out of the heinous business that was poaching. There were so many men and women who had done the same, if not worse, things as Peter. Sure, taking down Peter was personal for Ben, but he also wanted to end the poaching business altogether. He wanted people to stop torturing and killing animals for their own greed.

Ben had devised a plan that he could not stop with Peter. He had to take them all down, or there would be no use. Now, standing in front of the very people whom he hated the most, Ben felt like he was so close to his destiny. He could see everyone's face and wanted to tell them that he was coming for them. He wanted to point them out, one by one, and tell them that they were all going to hell. Ben could not do anything at the moment, though. So, he remained quiet and let Peter speak.

"Anyways, now it is time for me to retire urgently since I did promise Ben to give him a tour of my new place. You people can carry on. Have fun!" Peter said, then walked out of the ballroom.

Ben, Dana, and Jill were made to sit inside a limo along with Peter, with his gunmen pointing their weapons at each of them and letting them know that one wrong move would be their last move.

Peter kept smirking throughout the ride as the three sat in tense silence. Suddenly, he broke the silence by addressing Ben.

"So, Ben," Peter said. "Why is it that I have managed to get under your skin so much? How did that happen?"

Ben just stared at the man he hated with a passion and had to bite down on his tongue to not lash out against his restraints.

Jill and Dana looked at each other, then at Ben, not knowing how much longer Ben could control his anger.

"The jungle safari. Kenya. 1999. Ring a bell?" Ben said without any emotion in his voice.

To anyone else listening, Ben would've sounded almost bored or not interested, but to people who knew him, like Jill, they knew that Ben had reached the limit of his anger. That was when Ben became almost robotic in his mannerisms.

Peter frowned and looked like he was thinking hard. Then he looked up at Ben with a confused look on his face, "I can't remember. But honestly, I've been on so many safaris and in so many jungles that I can't remember any of them particularly."

Ben clenched his fists tightly, trying to rein in his anger.

"How can you not remember slaying a lion in front of a child?! How many times have you done something like that to forget about it? How are you so inhumane?" Ben yelled.

"Look, Ben," Peter leaned forward and said lightly. "Don't take it personally, but I honestly don't remember it. Are you sure it wasn't all just a dream?" Peter chuckled and reclined back in his seat.

Ben almost jumped forward in his seat, but the man pointing his gun at his head shoved him back in his seat.

"Ben, Ben, Ben," Peter said. "No need to get so antsy and frustrated. I am just trying to make conversation here. No need to make the girls here anxious with your aggressive behavior. Am I right, ladies?"

Jill just gave him the stink eye, and Dana rolled her eyes and looked away.

After that, the entire car ride was spent in silence, as Jill thanked God for Peter not speaking again and antagonizing Ben further.

The ride took longer than Ben would have expected, which made him think they were heading out of the city. Soon, they arrived on location as Peter and the men urged them to get out of the car. The three were herded inside a building after being blindfolded. Ben didn't like it one bit, but as long as the girls were with him, he couldn't make any rash moves. They walked for a long time and took many turns and twists that Ben could hardly tell the direction they were going in.

After being ushered inside a room, the three were made to sit on chairs. The men tied their feet to the chair legs and their hands behind their backs. It was a very painful and uncomfortable position to be in.

"You bastard! At least let the girls go! They haven't done anything! Your problem is with me!" Ben screamed.

Suddenly, their blindfolds were taken off, and they all blinked when they were attacked with the bright light of a bulb hanging above their heads. The room they were in looked like a typical kidnapper's basement. The walls were concrete and bare, with one light bulb illuminating the space. There were only three chairs. There was one door and no windows, Ben noticed with surmounting panic. He also expected Peter to say something more, but after tying the three to the chairs, Peter and his men left the room promptly.

Jill's face was marked with tear streaks, while Dana remained stoic. Ben felt frustrated and angry that they had been dragged into such a situation because of him. He had promised Jill and himself that he would get them out safely. Now they were stuck inside Peter's basement in some secret location, with no hopes of getting out.

Two entire nights went by like that as the three were kept tied to the chairs. They were given one water bottle per day to share with each other. Ben made sure he let the girls have more, not caring much about himself. He just wanted to get them out. Then he could take care of Peter on his own. Surprisingly, Jill had remained quiet the entire time. Ben figured it was because she was in shock. Then after two days had passed by, she spoke up.

"We'll be leaving today," she said out of the blue. Her voice was calm, and her face didn't show any signs of panic.

Ben just stared at her in confusion, wondering if he should be worried about her mental state. "What do you mean, Jill?"

"Before we came here, I left a message for Stan and his team. I told him that if I didn't contact him through the same IP address in two days, he should come for us. I sent him the location of the hotel and am pretty sure he can track us here from there," Jill explained.

Ben and Dana just stared at her in shock. "What? You called Stan? How do you know he would even come?"

"Ben, please, he dislikes you for the moment, not me. Of course, he would come. We're getting out today, don't worry," she said with so much surety that Ben had to believe her.

"Jill, I don't want to sound like I doubt your skills, but how would he find us here? We don't even know where we are," Dana pointed out.

"Because I left my tracker in Peter's limo," Jill said smugly. Then she explained to them that she had a tracker on herself when she came to rescue Dana, knowing that things could go sideways any moment, so she went prepared that time. Then when they were in Peter's car, she had dropped it there so Stan could come for them easily.

"Oh, my God, Jill! You are a genius!" Ben exclaimed.

Just as he said that, there was a sudden loud bang outside the room, the walls shook, and the light bulb flickered.

"Is that an earthquake?" Dana asked in fear.

"I believe that is Stan," Jill said.

For an hour, they could only hear loud bangs, bullets going off constantly, and the yells of different people. It sounded like utter chaos as if the war had broken outside the room. Then, suddenly, the door burst open, and it was one of Peter's men. He was bleeding from his head and looked worse for wear. He held a gun in his hand, and just as he took a step inside the room, a shot went off, and Dana jumped. The guy was shot in the head from the back, and Jill turned her head away, fearing she might throw up. The man fell to the ground like a sack of potatoes, and then they could see Stan in the doorway.

"You have come!" Jill said excitedly.

"Of course," Stan grunted.

He quickly came inside the room and quietly untied the three. Then he told them to wait and went to check if the path was clear. He peeked inside the hallway and shot once to the left. Then he yelled, "Clear!" and the three started moving. Stan handed Ben and Dana a gun each.

"Sorry, Jill, I know you don't like guns," Stan said.

"That's okay," Jill said, looking a little green as she walked out of the room and noticed the number of men lying and bleeding on the floor outside. It was a massacre.

"My men are outside, guarding the truck. Run! Now! I'll give you cover!" Stan commanded.

Ben walked in front, Jill right behind him, and then Dana and Stan bringing up the rear. They moved like one unit, shooting any of Peter's men they came across. Every time, Jill would wince and close her eyes, not willing to see her friends shooting people. She pretended she was in a VR video game so that she didn't stop and have a breakdown right then and there.

"Ben! On your left!" Stan yelled from the back while Ben was busy shooting two guys on his right.

Before Ben could turn around and take aim, Dana shot the man square in the head, and he fell with a thud.

"What? I have practice," Dana said as the rest of them turned to look at her in shock.

The group moved through the maze of hallways, picking out Peter's men one by one. The hallway lights were flickering, water flooding the path as a result of the grenades Stan's team had dropped on the place.

"What, did you guys nuke this place?" Ben asked, shocked at how the building seemed to be falling apart.

"Something like that," Stan said.

As they kept walking the hallways, they finally reached the exit door that led right outside. After opening the steel door, Dana walked out and informed the group that she could see Stan's men with the truck outside. Ben told them to make a run for it.

"No! We're not leaving you behind!" Jill said.

"You're not. I just need more time to find Peter and finish this thing once and for all," he said, holding her by the shoulders.

Jill shook her head, but Stan spoke up then, "He's right. We need to finish this off."

"I'll stay with you," Dana said, reloading her gun.

"No, I need you to go with Jill and give her protection. She can't fight; you can," Ben said.

"Ben," Dana said, hesitant to agree. She had tears in her eyes.

Ben couldn't help himself then. He lunged forward and embraced her tightly. He whispered, "I'm just glad we got you back safe."

Dana sobbed in his arms, and then he pulled back. He planted a soft kiss on her forehead and then lips. She kept her eyes closed, a few tears leaking past her lids. Jill and Stan looked away to give the two some privacy. Then Ben pushed Dana away gently, urging her to go. She didn't want to, but she knew Jill needed her protection. Their hands stayed connected until the very last moment, and then Dana turned and walked out the door. Ben hugged Jill, and she cried too.

"I don't want to leave you. I just know you'll do something stupid or heroic, or both," she whimpered.

"I promise I won't put myself in unnecessary danger," Ben assured her.

"Pinky promise?" Jill put out her pinky, and Ben chuckled.

He connected his pinky with hers, saying, "Pinky promise."

Jill wiped tears from her face and then walked out behind Dana. Ben and Stan stood watching, making sure the girls reached the truck safely, and then they closed the door. Ben's heart felt heavy as if that was his final goodbye. He didn't want to think about it, but what if that was the last time he saw them? He shook off his miserable thoughts and then walked with Stan as they made their way toward Peter. Now he just had to find that son of a bitch.

The hallways all looked the same, but somehow Stan knew where to go. Ben was glad he had Stan with him. He shuddered to think how differently this could have ended, especially with the girls. They made their silent, careful path through the heap of bodies and blood that was left behind. The sight was truly macabre, but Ben figured it was the collateral for their mission. He didn't like taking a human life, but he was left with no option. He couldn't sacrifice himself or any one of his team members.

"Do you know where he is, or we're just lost?" Ben whispered.

"Shhh! Stay quiet. And yes, I know where he is. I saw him," Stan whispered back.

Ben listened to him, and they walked ahead. After so much noise of gunshots, grenades, and people screaming and dying, the place was suddenly quiet. Too quiet. Had they killed everyone?

"They're hiding," Stan whispered, and Ben wondered if he had read his mind.

They traversed through the silent hallways until Stan stopped at another steel door.

"He's here," Stan whispered.

Ben mustered up all the anger and rage that had been festering inside him since he was a kid. He took a step ahead, but Stan stopped him.

"We can't just barge in like that! He probably has guns all around him!" Stan warned Ben.

Ben was too far gone to understand the logic at that point, though. "I'm going in. If you don't want to, you can stay."

Without another word, Ben shot at the lock and kicked the door open with a huge bang. Stan sighed and then followed Ben inside. Immediately, he spotted Peter hiding away in the corner like the coward he was. Ben was only focused on Peter, but Stan made sure to scout the entire room for any hidden threats. He spotted one man hiding underneath a table and immediately shot him dead. Ben didn't even flinch. He stepped forward and punched Peter squarely across the face.

"Shit!" Peter spat out blood through his mouth as he gripped his pained face.

Ben punched him in the gut, and Peter folded like the weak man he was. However, what Ben was not expecting was that Peter had hidden a weapon. He quickly pulled out a knife and ran at Ben with a mad look on his bleeding face. Ben's eyes widened, and before he could even aim his gun at Peter in defense, Stan pushed him to the side. Ben fell to the floor just as he watched Peter plunge the dagger into Stan's meaty arm. Stan groaned, but he still grabbed Peter by the throat using his other hand.

"You son of a bitch! You're gonna regret that!" Stan groaned.

Peter dropped the knife and held Stan's arm as he was choked. Ben watched the entire thing in shock, especially since Stan was still bleeding from his knife wound. Then, Peter reached out and punched Stan in the wound he had inflicted, and Stan let go of him with a scream. He coiled away from Peter as he kept hitting Stan in his hurt arm. Ben got up and pounced on Peter, throwing him away from Stan. Stan stumbled back and leaned against the door, sliding to the ground and holding his arm with a pained groan leaving his mouth. The blood was flowing out of his open wound profusely, and Ben knew he needed to stop that.

Ben punched Peter squarely across the face again and then hit him with the butt of his gun, making him fall to the floor and moan in pain. Ben quickly ran to Stan's side and grabbed his arm to inspect the wound, but Stan pushed him away.

"Don't," Stan groaned, his eyes closed and face twisted in pain. "Just go deal with him. You're the only one who can. Don't let him go again."

Ben just stared at Stan, but he refused to leave the man like that, or else he would bleed to death. Ben suddenly started unbuckling his belt and pulled it out of the loops. He immediately tied the belt around Stan's arm, right above his wound, and tied it tight enough to make the blood stop flowing out.

"Keep pressure on that," Ben told Stan.

Before Stan could reply, there was a sudden attack on Ben as Peter stood up and charged at him. Stan felt bad that he couldn't help him during such a tough time. He was slowly losing consciousness too. Peter came up from behind and started choking Ben with his arm. Ben struggled and tried to claw his arm off that was blocking his airways.

"You want to kill me?" Peter said through gritted teeth as he put in all his force to choke Ben. "You can try, but you'll fail."

Ben couldn't breathe, and his face was turning from red to purple. He was moving his hands around wildly, but Peter didn't stop. Then Ben realized that he had placed his gun down beside Stan's knee on the ground when he came to tend to his wound. He looked down and saw it still there. Ben tensed his body and then reached behind him with his right arm, grabbing Peter's knee and getting the leverage he needed to make Peter stumble and loosen his grip on his throat.

Peter stumbled, and Ben took the advantage to jump away and out of his grasp. He doubled down on Peter and kicked him in the back and the knees to make him go sprawling on the floor. Then Ben reached for his gun quickly and pointed it at Peter's face just as he turned his body and looked up at Ben. Peter's eyes widened when he saw Ben aiming the gun down at him. Then he started pleading for his life.

"Please, Ben. Please. Don't shoot me. I'll leave this business; I'll leave the country! I promise! Please, don't shoot me!" Peter had started crying pathetically as he begged Ben to spare his life.

Ben kept staring down at Peter, the man who had been responsible for all the anger and misery in Ben's life since so long ago. He stared at the man who had seemed so invulnerable and powerful before. Now, he was reduced to tears and snot, lying on the floor, bleeding, and at Ben's mercy. It was quite pathetic, really. Ben also knew that Peter must be killed for his doings. Ben could shoot Peter, and no one would know. Case closed. Ben would get rid of his enemy, and the world would be a better place. He kept staring down the barrel at Peter's crying face and put his thumb on the trigger.

Then again, Ben was a doctor. He had taken an oath to protect all life on earth, whether good or bad. He was a man responsible for saving lives, not ending them. He couldn't, in good conscience, kill Peter, even if he was the lowest of the lowest scum on this planet. He would never be able to live with himself after that. If he pulled that trigger, there would be no difference between him and Peter anymore. He would be stooping as low as him and turning into him. That was the last thing he wanted. Slowly, Ben lowered his arm, and Peter stared at him in shock. He couldn't believe he had been spared.

"The only sentence you will receive will be the one in court," Ben stated with finality.

***

In the darkroom, only the bright glow of the computer screen was visible. Ben's face was illuminated by the light, making his frown appear deeper. He was back inside his secret room, even though he had already caught and brought Peter to justice. His poaching business had dissolved, and his friends had all left him behind. Peter was as good as dead. Though, there was still something that nagged Ben. It was a weird sensation as if he had forgotten something important and just couldn't remember.

Ben scrolled the screen, looking at the names and information regarding all the men who were involved with Peter in his business. They had all been caught, one way or another. Mostly thanks to Dana. Then, as he reached the end of the list, he paused. The mouse pointer hovered over the name "Black Castle" on the screen. There was no other information listed because neither Jill nor Ben could find anything on it. At first, Ben thought it was the name of one of Peter's locations or the name of his mission, maybe. Then, throughout the whole journey of catching Peter, he had never once referred to anything as Black Castle. Honestly, Ben had forgotten about it. Now that he looked at it again, he couldn't help but wonder.

Who or what is Black Castle? What does it have to do with Peter and his business?

Yet, the biggest question remained.

Is it really over?

Did you know?

Most poaching is done by organized crime syndicates that use high-powered technology and weaponry to hunt and kill animals without being detected.

BRANDON KIMBROUGH

www.ingramcontent.com/pod-product-compliance
Lightning Source LLC
Chambersburg PA
CBHW060314030426
42336CB00011B/1035